Magnify

Magnify

The Pursuit of Glorifying the Lord

TREVOR LINDELL

RESOURCE *Publications* · Eugene, Oregon

MAGNIFY
The Pursuit of Glorifying the Lord

Resource Publications
An Imprint of Wipf and Stock Publishers
199 W. 8th Ave., Suite 3
Eugene, OR 97401

www.wipfandstock.com

PAPERBACK ISBN: 978-1-6667-8511-1
HARDCOVER ISBN: 978-1-6667-8512-8
EBOOK ISBN: 978-1-6667-8513-5

VERSION NUMBER 05/29/24

Contents

Acknowledgments

To Jesus: It's wild that you willingly died so that you could be near me forever. Thank you for giving me life. I can't wait to dwell with you for eternity.

To my wife and best friend, Madison: This would not have been possible without your unceasing support, willingness to listen to me ramble as I process things of God, laughing at my silly jokes, and for calling me higher when I fall short. I'll never get used to the fact that I get to do life with you. I love you.

To the brothers and sisters in Christ that walked alongside me throughout this journey: Words can't express how grateful I am for you all. Thank you for cheering me on, encouraging me, sharpening my theology, and reading through some very early and very rough drafts.

Disclaimer

OVER THE COURSE OF my walk with the Lord, he has frequently shown me that much of what I was historically taught by others about who he is just isn't true. God made it very clear that my understanding of him was led astray by people's opinions (including my own) rather than the truth of the Bible. To preface, this book will not be a critique of any religion, denomination, preacher, etc. The reality of the situation is, however, that every church and spiritual organization is filled with imperfect, sinful people. Sometimes, these people say things that are not in line with the truths of God and, when believed as a whole, can develop a mindset that the larger Christian culture submits to which can be dangerous and hinder our understanding of God's true character.

We live in a world where immediate gratification is a driving force for much that we do. Whether it be our phones giving us access to everything we need in a moment's notice, indulging in quick-fix activities, or struggling to follow through with long-term goals, we quickly latch on to things that provide a hasty result and struggle to wade through those bits of life that require patience. Not only do we cling to the immediate, but we also live in a culture that elevates the popular voice. We are quick to believe what is said by the celebrity, person in charge, governmental official, and figure on the pulpit. We would rather be told what to believe by someone in power who speaks about things we agree with rather than put in the hard work to encounter a truth that might challenge us.

These two things together create a recipe for disaster when it comes to being grown in the realities of the Lord. Sanctification, or the process of being made holy, takes our entire life, which does not appeal to our desire to be instantly gratified. In Phil 1:6, Paul declares that he is confident *"that he who began a good work in you will carry it on to completion until the day of Christ Jesus."* The thought of having to wait on God to finish his work in us all the way up until we meet him face to face can be very troubling. Due to our lack of patience with this process, many of us cling to the teaching of the preacher on the pulpit, the worship singer at the concert, or the friend in the coffee shop. Rather than spending consistent time in prayer and letting God do his transformative work in our hearts and minds as we should be, we are prone to receive from culture and our surroundings. I am by no means calling us to be overly critical about who we listen to and to never trust anyone who talks about Jesus. We absolutely should be careful, as *"the heart is deceitful above all things and without cure"* (Jer 17:9), but sway too far into criticality and you stand in the way of what God designed the fellowship of the believers to be, namely, a body who edifies and sharpens one another daily based on trust and a common sharing in the Spirit. I am challenging us to fight to believe the Bible first and foremost and to let everything else filter through that. I am challenging us to ponder whether we have been quick to believe someone who may have taken a verse or text out of context to sound appealing. I am challenging us to be consistently in prayer and to saturate ourselves in God's word every day. This is the key to unlocking a deeper understanding of the character of God, which will in turn enhance our joy.

We really do have an uphill battle here. We live in a society that tells us to receive specific information a certain way, and from certain people. We fall prey to hearing what we want to hear and disregarding the rest. We also have an enemy, the devil, who *"prowls around like a roaring lion looking for someone to devour"* (1 Pet 5:8), working in the shadows to convince us of untruths. The apostle Paul understood this type of culture when he declares in 2 Tim 4:3–4, *"For the time will come when people will not put up with sound doctrine. Instead, to suit their own desires, they will gather around them a great number of teachers to say what their itching ears want to hear. They will turn their ears away from the truth and turn aside to myths."* It is heartbreaking to God when someone believes a "truth" that isn't absolute truth, simply because "it just makes sense" or "my pastor said so" without ever actually opening their Bible to see if it is valid theology. If we believe man (who is by nature flawed) quicker than we believe God and his word, we are in for a heap of trouble. God is gracious in providing resources to us such as books, pastors, and worship music, but a resource should never be foundational to us. Full life, as laid out in John 10:10, comes exclusively from the true character of Jesus, not from what someone else has interpreted or believed.

All this being said, my hope in writing this book is not to present you with my opinions on specific Christian beliefs (which are flawed due to my sinful nature), but to point us to the larger picture that is painted throughout God's word. I am not God. God is God. I am just a broken man, pieced together by the King, striving to bring the truth of who he is to this broken world. I ask you not to read this book out of a place of consumption, but rather stimulation. Let this add fuel to the fire that propels you into a deeper understanding and love of God. This book by no means should replace the source of where you receive truth: the Bible. My prayer is that this book would be a supplement to you that encourages an enhanced revelation of the beauty and supremacy of the King. In everything that I write throughout this book, I encourage you to hold it up to Scripture and fact check it with the Bible.

Introduction

I GREW UP IN a family that has always been "religious" in the sense that we would refer to ourselves as people who believed in God and even went to church. The issue was my faith had no substance to it at all. It was shallow. It didn't challenge or grow me. It was based on things other than Christ alone. After the Lord rescued me from a season of depression due to circumstance, I began to see the true beauty of my Savior. I was graced with the ability to be surrounded by brothers and sisters in Christ who were serious about this whole "following Jesus" thing. I learned that being a Christian meant more than having good morals and embracing a title. As I then began to fall more and more in love with the Lord and his word, I became increasingly more perplexed by the fact that there were so many crucial pieces of being a follower of Jesus that I had never heard of before. Thanks to God, throughout college I was in a youth ministry that worked with high school students. In doing this, my heart would constantly break because of this one reality: many kids (and people in general; me included) have an extremely skewed view of who God is and who they are and, in turn, are being led into further desolation. I desperately wanted them to know the truth of the gospel so that they would encounter real joy. Out of this, God began to grow my heart for the contents of this book.

I want to begin this journey by making one thing abundantly clear: this book exists solely by God's grace. If left to my own devices, I would not have chosen to write this book. I am not a writer or even much of a reader. For this reason, it took me many months to get over my stubbornness and to engage with what the Lord was leading me into. Now, looking back over the course of this season he has ushered me through, I believe I understand why he did it. I could not have imagined the depths of his truth that this journey would thrust me into. If this book never saw the light of day, it would still be a worthwhile endeavor if for no other reason than that the Lord used this book to enable me to worship him more intimately. Since day one, I have felt that my time writing with the Lord, the author of life, has been an immeasurable gift, regardless of any readers he may bring to these pages. What an incredible adventure he has taken me on.

With that in mind, this is a book for people like me: the Christian man or woman doing their best to honor the King in word, deed, and desire. It is for people who yearn to know and love God with greater passion. This is for the people, myself included, who wish to stand before the Lord someday and hear, "*Well done, good and faithful servant! You have been faithful with a few things; I will put you in charge of many things. Come and share your master's happiness!*" (Matt 25:23).

My prayer over you, reader, is that after engaging with this book you would be able to walk away with a deeper understanding of three truths:

1. We hinder our own ability to rightly encounter the Lord because we struggle to see ourselves in a proper light. Our entitlement and pride pull us away from seeing who we really are and what we really deserve.

2. The Lord operates out of both the fullness of love and fullness of wrath at all times (although, as we will discuss, they manifest themselves differently when it comes to the believer and the nonbeliever). If we focus too heavily on one of these truths but neglect the other, it diminishes the weight of Jesus on the cross.

3. Both our ministry and worship can become drastically transformed for the betterment of God's glory and our joy when

we allow the truths he gives us to dictate the way we think, act, and feel.

As God has continued to grow me in these three specific areas, my heart for him has expanded exponentially. I realized that as I understood more of who I am, and who God is, the cross appeared increasingly more beautiful. As we begin this trek into a few of the intricacies of God, let us saturate our souls in prayer and open our hearts to allow the Spirit to transform us as he sees fit. Come and *"magnify the Lord with me, and let us exalt his name together!"* (Ps 34:3).

Chapter One

The Magnifying Glass

I will bless the Lord at all times; his praise shall continually be in my mouth. My soul makes its boast in the Lord; let the humble hear and be glad. Oh, magnify the Lord with me, and let us exalt his name together!

—PSALM 34:1–3

AS A KID, I was fascinated by magnifying glasses. I remember going outside on a hot, sunny day and lining up a magnifying glass perfectly between a leaf and the sun and watching as the rays homed in on a point of the leaf, causing it to burn. At the time it felt like I was doing some sort of magic trick. Little did I know I was using this object for the exact opposite purpose it was designed for. Rather than making something appear larger, as we understand magnifying glasses to do, it was being used for minimization. I was taking something very large (the sun) and causing it to shrink down into something smaller (the pinpointed ray on the leaf).

If there is one thing I have noticed we as the church do too frequently it's that we take something very large (the Lord), and cause it to shrink down into something smaller. It's time that we flip the script (back to its original design). We exist to take something infinitely large (the Lord) and endeavor to make it bigger by being a living magnifying glass for all to see through. In Rom 12:1–2, Paul urges us as believers *"in view of God's mercy, to offer your bodies as a living sacrifice, holy and pleasing to God—this is your true and proper worship. Do not conform to the pattern of this world, but be transformed by the renewing of your mind. Then you will be able to test and approve what God's will is—his good, pleasing and perfect will."* The definition of sacrifice is to offer up something of value for the glorification of another thing that is of higher value. So then, what Paul is calling us to do is be such sacrifices to the Lord that when someone sees us, they see *"Christ in [us], the hope of glory"* (Col 1:27).

My hope throughout this journey is to encourage us to be just that: magnifying glasses for the Lord. We will start with an examination into who we are according to God's word and how we have so frequently strayed away from the truth due to our sin. As we come into an understanding of who we are, we will then discuss who God is. There is an infinitely wide gap presented in Scripture (as we will come to see) between our inherent unworthiness and God's inherent worthiness. If we hope to come to a place where we can fully glorify the Lord in all ways, it will be hinged upon an initial belief that *"he must become greater; I must become less"* (John 3:30).

During the Sermon on the Mount in Matt 5:14–16, Jesus gives us insight into our purpose: *"You are the light of the world. A town built on a hill cannot be hidden. Neither do people light a lamp and put it under a bowl. Instead they put it on its stand, and it gives light to everyone in the house. In the same way, let your light shine before others, that they may see your good deeds and glorify your Father in heaven."* What Jesus is trying to portray to us is that we are to be a magnifying glass. We allow the light of Christ to shine brightly within us so that what people will really see is God's magnificence and be led to glorify him.

The prophet Isaiah had an encounter with the Lord in Isa 6:1–8 that transformed the way he understood himself and God. Let's take a look and see how his transformation can lead to a deeper revelation regarding our purpose:

> *In the year that King Uzziah died, I saw the Lord, high and exalted, seated on a throne; and the train of his robe filled the temple. Above him were seraphim, each with six wings: With two wings they covered their faces, with two they covered their feet, and with two they were flying. And they were calling to one another:*
>
> *"Holy, holy, holy is the Lord Almighty;*
> *the whole earth is full of his glory."*
>
> *At the sound of their voices the doorposts and thresholds shook and the temple was filled with smoke.*
>
> *"Woe to me!" I cried. "I am ruined! For I am a man of unclean lips, and I live among a people of unclean lips, and my eyes have seen the King, the Lord Almighty."*
>
> *Then one of the seraphim flew to me with a live coal in his hand, which he had taken with tongs from the altar. With it he touched my mouth and said, "See, this has touched your lips; your guilt is taken away and your sin atoned for."*
>
> *Then I heard the voice of the Lord saying, "Whom shall I send? And who will go for us?"*
>
> *And I said, "Here am I. Send me!"*

This Scripture has stood out to me from the moment I first read it. I personally believe that it embodies the entirety of Christ's gospel, even before he came to Earth. But we tend to mix up the sequence of events in our heads too frequently. You see, before he even knows where he would be sent, Isaiah did not hesitate when he responds to the Lord with *"Here am I. Send me!"* That comes afterward when the Lord reveals to Isaiah that he will spend a great deal of time calling out people's lack of love for the Lord although they will not repent.

We tend to view Isaiah's calling (and our own callings) in this way:

1. An encounter with the Lord's presence
2. An acknowledgment of unworthiness and inherent brokenness before him
3. A transformation by his renewing and regenerative power
4. An insight as to where he will be sending
5. A decision as to whether or not to go

Do you see where we get it all wrong? Isaiah's heart was in a very different place than where we tend to let ours fester. The way that Isaiah encounters his calling (and perhaps the most submissive way for us to do so) is as follows:

1. An encounter with the Lord's presence
2. An acknowledgment of unworthiness and inherent brokenness before him
3. A transformation by his renewing and regenerative power
4. A commitment to go wherever the Lord decides
5. An insight as to where he will be sending

Isaiah had made up his mind to go where the Lord wanted him to go, not because of where he was being sent, but because of who was sending him. What a beautiful model Isaiah gives to us regarding submission to the Lord amid our purpose and calling. We have come into an encounter with the living God, have repented of our brokenness, and have been washed clean by the blood of Christ. Why then do we wait to decide if our calling suits us? Instead, out of humble submission, we ought to start our march forward and then let the Lord lay the path before us. True surrender to the Lord looks like going where he pleases, when he pleases, simply because he's worthy. The destination can never alter our drive in our pursuit of him.

As we all likely know, this is far easier said than done and is oftentimes just plain difficult. There are many things that get in the way of our willingness to follow regardless of the final earthly outcome. We often align with the disciple in Matt 8:21–22 when *"Another disciple said to him, 'Lord, first let me go and bury my father.' But Jesus told him, 'Follow me, and let the dead bury their own dead.'"* The things of this world that seem obligatory or provide comfort often get in the way of our ability to lay it all down at his feet. We want to make sure all our ducks are in a row before we fully commit to a life of glorifying the Lord regardless of the cost.

The Bible is one big book pointing directly at Christ on the cross. Now to be clear, throughout this book, when I reference the cross, I am not referring to the object, but rather the event. The cross is the summation of the power that is displayed and distributed by way of the blood of Christ. A piece of wood in the shape of a *t* does nothing. But the King of the universe, bearing our punishment, dying on our behalf, conquering death, ascending to Heaven, and imparting to his people the Holy Spirit? Now that is the cross. The whole point of the Bible is to glorify Jesus by walking as a reflection of his character. Not just the event of a guy dying on a tree, but what the death and resurrection of Jesus provided and accomplished. So, as we step into this journey together, let us open our hearts to where God wants to take us. Let us prayerfully come before him and allow him to refine the parts of our hearts that have hindered our ability to bring him maximized glory. This book will not change your heart in and of itself. But as you read, let the Lord speak to you through his word and prayer, changing your very being for the betterment of his name. Allow your life to be a magnifying glass to the world, that people would see the King magnified in and through you.

Chapter Two

The Centerpiece of Everything

The thief comes only to steal and kill and destroy; I have come that they may have life, and have it to the full.

—JOHN 10:10

LET'S START WITH A claim: We greatly hinder our capability of understanding the fullness of God's love due to our natural, sin-born entitlement. It took me many years to come to the realization that God didn't give us the Bible for our benefit, but rather his glory. This gets easily misconstrued because the pathway he chose to bring himself maximized glory is through providing to us the ability to experience maximized joy in him. This then leads us to fall into the trap of thinking that the Lord's primary motive is for us to have joy. John 10:10 is a wonderfully powerful verse about God's heart for his people, but we need the context to see the full picture. Jesus plops this verse right in the middle of his analogy about himself being the shepherd and us being the sheep.

The important thing to note is that the shepherd does not exist for the sheep, but rather the sheep for the shepherd. We see this very clearly in Gen 9:3 when God explains to Noah that *"Everything that lives and moves about will be food for you. Just as I gave you the green plants, I now give you everything."* From the very beginning, as depicted in Gen 2, God creates plants and animals for Adam's benefit. The beautiful aspect of Jesus's analogy is that he uses the image of us being sheep to elevate the power of him choosing to die for us, as stated in verse 11: *"I am the good shepherd. The good shepherd lays down his life for the sheep."* Sheep have historically been domesticated for the products they provide: meat, skin, milk, and wool. The shepherd does not take care of the sheep so that they will live a good life and go on their merry way apart from him. No, he cares for them so that he will in turn receive from them what they were created to do. So then, what separates Jesus, the Good Shepherd, from any other shepherd? He is the only one who was able to die for the sheep and yet still daily provide for them through his conquering of death.

So then, what does it mean for us to be Jesus's sheep? Why were we created, why did Jesus die and rise again, and why does God provide us full life and joy in him if not actually for our benefit alone? Thankfully, he provides a clear answer in Isa 43:1–7:

> *But now, this is what the Lord says—*
> *he who created you, Jacob,*
> *he who formed you, Israel:*
> *"Do not fear, for I have redeemed you;*
> *I have summoned you by name; you are mine.*
> *When you pass through the waters,*
> *I will be with you;*
> *and when you pass through the rivers,*
> *they will not sweep over you.*
> *When you walk through the fire,*
> *you will not be burned;*
> *the flames will not set you ablaze.*
> *For I am the Lord your God,*
> *the Holy One of Israel, your Savior;*
> *I give Egypt for your ransom,*

Cush and Seba in your stead.
Since you are precious and honored in my sight,
and because I love you,
I will give people in exchange for you,
nations in exchange for your life.
Do not be afraid, for I am with you;
I will bring your children from the east
and gather you from the west.
I will say to the north, 'Give them up!'
and to the south, 'Do not hold them back.'
Bring my sons from afar
and my daughters from the ends of the earth—
everyone who is called by my name,
whom I created for my glory,
whom I formed and made."

What a powerful image God provides. He gives everything for us, fights our battles, provides for our needs, gives us life, and delights in us, all so that we will do what we were created to do: give him all the glory. This radically flips our understanding of love on its head. God could not have loved us any better than by bringing us to himself. In a Bible study for high school students I used to lead, one of the kids once compared God to *The Giving Tree* (the 1964 book by Shel Silverstein). It took me a moment to realize that this was the way this student (as well as many other people) viewed love and, in turn, viewed God's love. We naturally encounter love as an outpouring of someone else onto us wherein the lover often experiences deficit through sacrifices for the loved. For example, parents experience a financial deficit when they lovingly pay for what their kids need (whether it be food, education, experiences, or the like). Take Jack Dawson's sacrifice in *Titanic* as another example. He very obviously experiences deficit when he displays his love for Rose by letting her survive on the floating door while he dies from the cold water. Many of us experience an emotional connection to this scene because, on a deeper level, this is how we view love: sacrifice by way of deficit. Not so with God. He is not "The Giving Tree" in the sense that he experiences deficit when he lovingly provides for his children. Rather, in loving his children, his glory and supremacy further grows.

How can this be? How is he able to give something away without losing anything at all? Well, God cannot lose financial standing through sacrifice and love, because *"to the Lord your God belong the heavens, even the highest heavens, the earth and everything in it"* (Deut 10:14). It is impossible for him to lose time through sacrifice and love, as *"with the Lord a day is like a thousand years, and a thousand years are like a day"* (2 Pet 3:8). Perhaps the most powerful proof of the Lord not experiencing deficit is found at the cross. The Father's sacrifice that was made for you and me did not lead to the loss of Jesus, the Son, but rather further elevated his own glory. Not even death is a deficit to him, as he makes clear in Rev 1:18: *"I am the Living One; I was dead, and now look, I am alive for ever and ever! And I hold the keys of death and Hades."* All in all, everything belongs to the one true King. Nothing he gives to us is ours permanently, as it is still under his jurisdiction, and he is able to use the resources he doles out as he sees fit.

In response to this, some may say: "So God is just selfish and using us for his own benefit?" Well, the short answer to that question is, not exactly. At least not in the way we view selfishness. If full life on Earth and eternal joy in Heaven are found exclusively in him, then it is an incredible gift that he created us with the sole purpose of worshiping and glorifying him. We experience full life by bringing him praise. Let's take another look at Scripture where God emphatically declares the purpose of his love in Hos 2:19-23:

> *"I will betroth you to me forever;*
> *I will betroth you in righteousness and justice,*
> *in love and compassion.*
> *I will betroth you in faithfulness,*
> *and you will acknowledge the Lord.*
> *"In that day I will respond,"*
> *declares the Lord—*
> *"I will respond to the skies,*
> *and they will respond to the earth;*
> *and the earth will respond to the grain,*
> *the new wine and the olive oil,*

and they will respond to Jezreel.
I will plant her for myself in the land;
I will show my love to the one I called 'Not my loved one.'
I will say to those called 'Not my people,' 'You are my people';
and they will say, 'You are my God.'"

God betroths and plants us for himself, and we would not want it any other way. The entire story of the Bible is about how we broke away from intimacy with the Father, turning to our own ways in sin. However, God was not content with this because his beloved children were not experiencing full life in him through glorification of himself, so he sent his Son to draw us back to himself in order for us to be in communion with him once again. He gets the praise and we get the "*boundless riches of Christ*" (Eph 3:8).

My wife Madison and I have a goldendoodle named Lulu. She is a bundle of happiness and energy and brings us both much joy. When Madison claimed ownership of Lulu prior to us being married, it was for that very reason: to bring her much joy. She loves animals and knew that a new pup would provide a benefit to her life. When Madison was on her way to the breeder, no one was faulting her for getting a dog to further enhance her own life. Rather, it's widely understood that we care for and love dogs so that they will put smiles on our faces when they give love in return (and we as humans tend to have a soft spot for cute, fluffy things).

God operates on a similar frequency. So, is he selfish for loving us unbelievably well (in caring for us, fighting for us, and sacrificing his Son for us) in order that we will love him with our whole being? Well, if we boil down what selfishness is to "primarily seeking one's own gain," then absolutely, God is selfish. But this is not selfishness in the same way that we define it. We view selfishness as one's gain in disregard for others. God is the only one who is able to perpetually seek his own gain while simultaneously caring for others. Just as we love dogs for their affection and shepherds love sheep for what they can produce, God loves us for his glory. He is the well of living water and therefore the only way to receive life is by going to him and drawing from the source. Praise him that he did not make us the centerpiece of his love story. Praise him for understanding that the key to our joy is lifting his name high and committing our whole selves to daily bringing him glory. Praise him for seeking first his own glory, that we may encounter life through it.

Pastor, theologian, and author John Piper, in an aim to illuminate a similar mindset, coined the term "Christian Hedonism." As laid out on his Desiring God ministry platform, "Christian Hedonism is the conviction that God's ultimate goal in the world (his glory) and our deepest desire (to be happy) are one and the same, because God is most glorified in us when we are most satisfied in him. Not only is God the supreme source of satisfaction for the human soul, but God himself is glorified by our being satisfied in him. Therefore, our pursuit of joy in him is essential."[1] What a powerful way of life to emulate. What a wonderful King we have that he should design us in such a way that he grows in glory as we grow in joy. Many kings throughout history have enhanced their own dominion through the deprivation of their servants. God, on the other hand, enhances his own dominion through the fulfillment and satisfaction of his servants.

This is the first step in our magnification of Christ on the cross. As we continue to allow the glorification of the Lord to be our chief motive, we concurrently make the cross larger and more evident in our lives. How then does our sin-born entitlement hinder our understanding of God? It takes away from our necessary commitment to making everything about God alone. "*He must become greater; I must become less*" (John 3:30). Are we positioning the magnifying glass over ourselves or our King? If I am "following God" to maximize my own life, then I'm not actually following the true God at all and will always fall short of wholeness. We have an ongoing battle against falling into the trap of thinking everything revolves around us. When this extends to God's character, we won't be able to effectively live out what he has called us to do throughout the Bible. Yet none of this considers the biggest reason why our entitlement hinders our understanding: we deserve nothing, yet he gives us everything.

1. Piper, "Christian Hedonism," §1.

Chapter Three

The Man on Death Row

For all have sinned and fall short of the glory of God, and all are justified freely by his grace through the redemption that came by Christ Jesus.

—ROMANS 3:23–24

For the wages of sin is death, but the gift of God is eternal life in Christ Jesus our Lord.

—ROMANS 6:23

IT IS QUITE SOBERING to hear these verses assert that I am a sinful man, and that what I perpetually earn is death. We don't naturally view ourselves as messed up, broken people, in daily need of a savior, yet this is precisely what we are. As we previously spoke about, we tend to deem ourselves as the primary focus of our own stories and aren't too keen on admitting we are actually the villain. "But I'm not *that* bad," one might say. "I'm not *nearly* as messed up as that person," says another. We want to be the good guy, the likable protagonist, and the hero, so we deflect our sinfulness onto others through comparison. "I may be no Mother Teresa, but I'm definitely no Hitler." The truth is, reader, that you, me, Mother Teresa, and Hitler have all earned the same wage for what we have done: death.

The letter of James is powerful for many reasons, but I believe that chief among these is how unapologetically James lays down the facts. In chapter 2 of his letter, as he is wrapping up his declaration that showing favoritism is sinful, he broadens the scope of the claim by saying, "*whoever keeps the whole law and yet stumbles at just one point is guilty of breaking all of it*" (Jas 2:10). Even the "littlest" of sins are equal to the largest iniquities when it comes to falling short of perfection. If perfection on an exam is scoring a 100 percent, then regardless of if you scored a 99 percent or a 0 percent, you were imperfect. That's really what sin is at the heart of it all: a falling short of the perfection that God originally designed for us to live out. Therefore, regardless if I lied about what I did over the weekend or committed murder, I am guilty of imperfection and sin. Now if what Paul says in Rom 6 is true, and the wage that we have earned for our sin is death, then it doesn't matter how bad we are. We inevitably deserve to die. At the end of the day, the truth of the matter is that I am no hero. I am not the good guy in the story. I am the villain and have done nothing in and of myself but break the law and break God's heart.

Our brains have a way of doing this wild thing where we assume that we are naturally good people. That if we were to die and go to hell, it would be because God took our deserved eternity in Heaven away from us and threw us into the depths. But the reality is quite the opposite. The entire point of the fall in Gen 3 is to show that *we* chose to distance ourselves from the Lord, creating a separation between us. If Heaven is eternity with the Father wherein all goodness dwells (Jas 1:17), then hell is simply eternity without the Father wherein there is no goodness, only misery. By choosing to not dwell with the Lord, we choose to live apart from him, which means we are on the pathway to an eternity void of his presence. You see, we are not deserving of Heaven and God sends us to hell.

We are inherently deserving of hell, death, and wrath, and God, in his abundant grace and love for those who submit to him, gives life, joy, and peace forever.

Our pride puts up a fight when we try to accept our brokenness, yet it is vital to our understanding and receiving the gifts of the Father. I spoke earlier of how our entitlement makes it difficult to grasp the fact that we deserve nothing but death, yet God himself gives us everything. Jesus Christ, God's only Son, died to save the sinner from the death they deserve. How can I be saved from something when I refuse to be in need of rescue? There is an old story about G. K. Chesterton (an early 1900s English author and theologian) that frames the reality of our situation. As the story goes, *The Times* of London published a question to Chesterton as well as other notable authors asking, "What is wrong with the world?" Chesterton responded very powerfully with "Dear Sir, regarding your article 'What is wrong with the world?' I am. Yours truly, G. K. Chesterton." While there is no officially documented evidence of this statement, we would do well to adopt this mindset. I, Trevor Lindell, am what is wrong with the world. I am by nature broken, wretched, and a plague to the world God originally designed for me to live in. If I fail to see myself as the problem, I'll never be able to truly receive the solution. This brings us to the primary issue that arises in our entitlement: We make the cross out to be incredibly small.

Let's say for a moment that there is a man on death row for repeatedly breaking the law. He knows he is guilty and deserving of the punishment as he sits in the electric chair, awaiting his death. Now let's say, right before the executioner does his job, Jesus busts through the door and says, "You are deserving of death, but I am here to take the punishment for you." Jesus is then killed in place of the man. Think about what this man would be feeling. There would be an overflow of incomprehensible joy and gratitude over what his Savior had done. He would live every day the rest of his life with his Savior in mind, knowing that he was given a new life at the expense of another.

Alternatively, let's look at another example. Take your average American man who lives a "normal" life. He has a wife and three kids, works an honest job, and even helps out around the community from time to time. He has not committed a crime that would warrant jail time or any legal punishment. People generally speak highly of him. Now let's say, while the man is having dinner with his family, Jesus busts through the door and says, "You are deserving of death, but I am here to take the punishment for you." Jesus is then killed in place of the man. Think about what *this* man would be feeling. He would likely be confused about what Jesus meant regarding his deserved death. Jesus paying the price for the man would not have meant much at all and the man's life could remain largely unchanged after the encounter.

Jesus himself backs up this comparison in Luke 7:41–43 when he says:

> *"Two people owed money to a certain moneylender. One owed him five hundred denarii, and the other fifty. Neither of them had the money to pay him back, so he forgave the debts of both. Now which of them will love him more?"*
>
> Simon replied, *"I suppose the one who had the bigger debt forgiven."*
>
> *"You have judged correctly,"* Jesus said.

We are very quick to see ourselves as the average man who is living the normal life or who only owed fifty denarii. We carry on with our business, trying to do good from time to time with our own moral compasses. We are aware of Christ's death on the cross, yet we diminish this power because of entitlement. We believe we are better people than we actually are and therefore deserve better than we actually do. The truth is, reader, you are the man on death row. I am the man on death row. You owe the moneylender an incomprehensible sum. You have daily broken God's laws and commands, and you await your deserved punishment. Yet Jesus came to your rescue and saved you. Now, we live on the other side of the cross, experiencing the washing and freedom that comes from our Lord. Oh, how life-changing the cross becomes when we receive the gift of Christ in this manner.

It is important to note that this reality of being freed is exclusive to the believer. In my introduction I noted that this book was written primarily for those who are born again Christians that have fully surrendered their lives to the King, and this is why. We are very quick in this modernized Western Christian theological world to extend God's forgiveness to those who are not forgiven. Let me be very upfront about this: the Bible is very clear that our being forgiven and washed of our guiltiness is only through a life that is renewed by the Holy Spirit through Christ on the cross. For us to declare that someone is forgiven when they are not of the body of Christ is to give false hope and to shed a false light on the Lord. Let's take a look at just a few of the many Scriptures that prove this.

John 3:16–18 is a widely used Scripture, but if we miss out on the specifics of the words used in the text, it will throw its entire meaning off track.

> *For God so loved the world that he gave his one and only Son, that whoever believes in him shall not perish but have eternal life. For God did not send his Son into the world to condemn the world, but to save the world through him. Whoever believes in him is not condemned, but whoever does not believe stands condemned already because they have not believed in the name of God's one and only Son.*

There is a clear distinction between those who are condemned and not condemned, and it's hinged exclusively on belief in Jesus. But we have to go deeper, because unfortunately "belief in Jesus" looks wildly different today than it did back then. This is why verses like Rom 10:9–10 have done a lot of harm to us: we take them out of context.

> *If you declare with your mouth, "Jesus is Lord," and believe in your heart that God raised him from the dead, you will be saved. For it is with your heart that you believe and are justified, and it is with your mouth that you profess your faith and are saved.*

These two texts together could lead the casual reader into thinking that if they simply believe that Jesus exists and verbally call themselves "Christians," they will be saved and have a ticket to Heaven when they die. More specifically, Rom 10:9–10 was never meant to be a one-time declaration, but rather a persistent heart posture until the Lord calls us home. If it were meant to be a one-time event, then why does Jesus make this claim in Matt 7:21–23:

> *Not everyone who says to me, "Lord, Lord," will enter the kingdom of heaven, but only the one who does the will of my Father who is in heaven. Many will say to me on that day, "Lord, Lord, did we not prophesy in your name and in your name drive out demons and in your name perform many miracles?" Then I will tell them plainly, "I never knew you. Away from me, you evildoers!"*

For the longest time this was one of the scariest texts in the Bible to me. But it's not meant to produce constant anxiety about whether or not we are saved. It's meant to give us a clearer picture into what it looks like *to* be saved. What Jesus is trying to express here is that nominal "Christians" (Christian in name alone), are not born-again brothers and sisters in Christ. Well then, what does it mean to "declare with your mouth, Jesus is Lord, and believe in your heart that God raised him from the dead"? This is where time frame and context come into play.

If I were to walk into my place of work today and declare, "I believe that Jesus is Lord," I may get some weird looks or a slap on the wrist. But, if I were to say this in first-century Rome, I would experience oppression ranging anywhere from public humiliation to death. Christians in Rome encountered fierce persecution for nearly three centuries under various Roman rulers, which even led to mass killings of believers under Emperor Decius in AD 250. Verbally exclaiming that Jesus is Lord back when Paul penned the letter to the Romans would be akin to what our brothers and sisters in various places in Asia and Africa are experiencing today where Christianity is illegal. If you are unfamiliar with what is happening in these areas, I highly recommend spending some time in research because it is truly profound what our brothers and sisters in Christ are enduring for the sake of the kingdom of God. They spend every day with an understanding that at any moment they could be beaten, raped, or murdered for being a Christian. There are many resources out there, such as the two-part *Sheep among Wolves* documentary, which help illuminate the faith of our overseas spiritual family. And for those of you who are living or have lived in the thick of this persecution in these areas, I say thank you. Your unyielding faithfulness to the Lord is such an encouragement to me and many others around the world.

All this to say that being a Christian in many modern cultures looks different than it used to, for better and for worse. We see that from history, claiming to be a Christian meant that you were whole-heartedly surrendered to the Father, you were willing to die at a moment's notice because Jesus is Lord, and you lived a life that was daily led by the Holy Spirit. Being a true biblical Christian goes so much further than just believing that a guy named Jesus existed. It means that you daily live your life in reverence and worship to the Lord as well as abiding by his word in Scripture. When Paul wrote in Eph 2:8 that "*it is by grace you have been saved, through faith—and this is not from yourselves, it is the gift of God,*" he understood that faith meant not just belief in the existence of God, but full trust and reliance on the person of Jesus.

I've always been bewildered by Paul's faith and confidence in the Lord. How can a man go through so much pain and hardship (see 2 Cor 11:16–33) yet still be able to say in Rom 8:18, "*I consider that our present sufferings are not worth comparing with the glory that will be revealed in us*"? Thankfully, Paul gives us the recipe to the secret sauce, as I refer to it, in his letter to the Philippian church:

> I know what it is to be in need, and I know what it is to have plenty. I have learned the secret of being content in any and every situation, whether well fed or hungry, whether living in plenty or in want. I can do all this through [Christ] who gives me strength. (Phil 4:12–13)

So, true biblical surrender, obedience, and strength comes from Jesus himself. This then brings us back full circle to the man on death row: us. Paul peels back the curtain to reveal the importance of understanding the price that was paid by Jesus on the cross. At this point, we have looked at the cross from a thirty-thousand-foot view. What we have not talked about is what is at stake for us, tangibly. We have not come to an understanding of how God feels within our sin and why the cross truly is infinitely tall and wide. We haven't yet talked about God's wrath.

Chapter Four

The Wrathful Father
Full of Love

Whoever believes in the Son has eternal life, but whoever rejects the Son will not see life, for God's wrath remains on them.

—JOHN 3:36

IF YOU HAVE BEEN following Jesus for any amount of time you are likely familiar with the story of Jesus in the garden of Gethsemane, shortly before he went to the cross. While there, he prayed "'*Abba, Father,' he said, 'everything is possible for you. Take this cup from me. Yet not what I will, but what you will'*" (Mark 14:36). This verse is generally something I have seen be used to demonstrate how we should submit to the Father's will. While this is true, there is another huge aspect that we tend to glance over: the cup. Why is Jesus agonizing in prayer to the point of sweating drops of blood? It's because he understood what "the cup" was, and what he was about to endure.

I want to paint a picture for you. Crucifixion is thought of as one of the most (if not *the* most) gruesome forms of punishment and execution. The Romans had nearly perfected it so that people would be driven away from breaking the law. To start, the convicted would undergo public trial and humiliation. Then, they would be flogged and whipped, all while experiencing constant verbal and physical abuse. Following that, they would carry the crossbeams (which weighed around one hundred pounds) to the site of execution. Once there, they would be nailed or tied to the cross and lifted up. It would take someone anywhere between hours and days to die in this way. Their cause of death would generally be from constrained blood circulation, organ failure, or asphyxiation (suffocation) from the body being strained under its own weight.

Jesus underwent all of this. He experienced the fullness of the crucifixion process and was largely silent through it all. In truth, this is in accordance with what was prophesied in Isa 53:7 when it was written that *"he was oppressed and afflicted, yet he did not open his mouth; he was led like a lamb to the slaughter, and as a sheep before its shearers is silent, so he did not open his mouth."* But his silence is also because there was one specific thing that caused Jesus to cry out:

> At noon, darkness came over the whole land until three in the afternoon. And at three in the afternoon Jesus cried out in a loud voice, "Eloi, Eloi, lema sabachthani?" (which means "My God, my God, why have you forsaken me?").
> When some of those standing near heard this, they said, "Listen, he's calling Elijah."
> Someone ran, filled a sponge with wine vinegar, put it on a staff, and offered it to Jesus to drink. "Now leave him alone. Let's see if Elijah comes to take him down," he said.
> With a loud cry, Jesus breathed his last.
> The curtain of the temple was torn in two from top to bottom. And when the centurion, who stood there in front of Jesus, saw how he died, he said, "Surely this man was the Son of God!" (Mark 15:33–39)

"The straw that broke the camel's back" in this instance was not the physical pain, but the spiritual pain. In this moment, Jesus was experiencing for the first time complete separation from the Father, in which he endured the entirety of the debt that we owed. So, what then is the cup in the garden referring to, and what did Jesus truly encounter? It is the fullness of God's wrath. We know this because when Jesus uses the word "forsake" he is saying that God has abandoned him.

This is where we get some of the aspects of theology that I misunderstood in my early walk with the Lord. I, alongside many others that I've met, always thought of God as powerful, but only ever exhibiting love. I know some people who even take it as far as believing that God *only* loves, and therefore no one goes to hell. We tend to view Jesus as this weak-kneed fellow who sits around petting lambs while sharing stories with kids rather than the warrior who doesn't tolerate spiritual nonsense as he flips tables, whips people, and calls some of them a *"brood of vipers"* (Matt 12:34). As we move forward, there is something vital that we need to understand: the Lord is just. He is the full embodiment of love as well as wrath. One hundred percent love and one hundred percent wrath, at all times, without fail. While Jesus is definitely not weak-kneed, he is absolutely gentle and tender-hearted. While Jesus is definitely not a tyrant ruler, he is absolutely a fighter and exhibits anger in a holy way. The Father is one in the same. As Paul says in Col 1:15 *"The Son is the image of the invisible God, the firstborn over all creation."* While the Father doles out love in droves, he is also a jealous God who is not slow to punishing those who oppose him. Don't believe me? Look at the cross. What better picture of simultaneous love and wrath could ever exist? God has such immense love for his people that he chose to pour out the wrath he had toward them onto his Son so that we could be with him.

It's also important to note that the wrath of God, while ever present in our world today, was not around when the original blueprint for humanity was made reality. As D. A. Carson wonderfully explains in his book *The Difficult Doctrine of the Love of God*:

> In itself, wrath, unlike love, is *not* one of the intrinsic perfections of God. Rather, it is a function of God's holiness against sin. Where there is no sin, there is no wrath—but

there will always be love in God. Where God in his holiness confronts his image-bearers in their rebellion, there *must* be wrath, or God is not the jealous God he claims to be, and his holiness is impugned. The price of diluting God's wrath is diminishing God's holiness.[1]

There will come a day in the not-so-distant future when God's wrath will no longer exist. He will come and redeem his people once and for all and bring them into perfect harmony with him on the New Earth as laid out in the book of Revelation. But until then, sin ravages on, and therefore his wrath continues its fight against all sin and darkness in order to preserve his innate holiness and righteousness. You may be wondering what implications this has on how we should view our own sin. Well, you'll just have to wait until chapter 10 for us to sink our teeth into that area.

I think the reason we tend to fall short in understanding the wrath of God comes from our lack of knowledge of its biblical inclusion. For good reason, new believers will often be pointed in the direction of reading the New Testament, as knowing the person of Jesus is vital to our faith. The drawback with doing this is that the New Testament is primarily written with God's wrath having already been placed onto his Son. Jesus came to us in human form in order to free us from our debt that bound us to wrath, which is explained to us in the four Gospels and the book of Acts. Beyond that, most of the Epistles (letters to churches) were written specifically to believers who, by way of the cross, were not under God's wrath anymore. Paul very explicitly lays this reality out in his letter to the church of Colossae (Col 1:21–22):

> *Once you were alienated from God and were enemies in your minds because of your evil behavior. But now he has reconciled you by Christ's physical body through death to present you holy in his sight, without blemish and free from accusation.*

What a beautiful truth! Because of Christ on the cross, the Lord no longer looks at you and me with any wrath. He sees us as holy and without blemish, showing us exclusively the fullness of his

1. Carson, *Difficult Doctrine*, 67.

love. We are no longer alienated from him but are his sons and daughters. Now, I want to be clear about something as we move forward: God the Father, God the Son (Jesus), and God the Holy Spirit, whom we tend to refer to as "the Trinity," are on the same page relating to all things. Christ was not only loving, the Father was not only wrathful, and the Holy Spirit was certainly not just some real life rendition of Casper the Friendly Ghost. Christ is just as loving as the Father and the Holy Spirit. He is also just as wrathful as the Father and the Holy Spirit. But don't take my word for it. Spend some time studying scriptures such as 1 Cor 8:6, 2 Cor 3:17, Col 2:9, John 10:30, or the many others for proof that the Triune God is one in eternality, divinity, character, will, and mind.

If we only ever read the New Testament, we wouldn't ever get the whole picture of God's character. It took me years to really dive into the Old Testament because it felt daunting and confusing. This was largely due to how much it seemed to go against the God that I knew in the New Testament. But what God came to open my eyes to (and what I pray he opens your eyes to) is that he is no less loving in the Old Testament and he is no less wrathful in the New Testament. I came to realize that understanding his wrath is the key to fully appreciating his love.

Let's circle back to the cup that Jesus references in the garden of Gethsemane. When Jesus pleads with God to take the cup from him, he is referencing Jer 25:15–38 in which God explains that this *"cup filled with the wine of [his] wrath"* will be consumed by anyone who is not his people. The rest of the passage lays out terrible things that will happen to all who drink from it, yet it is inescapable. But the prophecy doesn't stop there. Out of God's grace, he provides to us Isa 51:17–23 in which he declares that not only have you drunk from this cup, but that he has taken it out of your hand so that *"you will never drink again."* Then we see in Isa 52 and 53 the prophecy that Jesus will come to be the one to take the cup from us once and for all. God's wrath is gruesome. His hatred for sin is incomprehensible. His disgust for the ungodly is staggering. Yet he was willing to pour the entirety of it out onto his Son for the sake of you being with him.

As much of the New Testament is focused on God's love that is given to his children, much of the Old Testament is focused on God's wrath and anger poured out onto his enemies as he obliterates them and wipes them off the map in order to preserve righteousness and what he wills for his people. Let's take a look at three passages that give a clear picture of how God feels about those who are not living for him: Ps 11:5–7, 1 Thess 5:9–10, and Mal 1:2–3.

PSALM 11:5–7

The Lord examines the righteous,
but the wicked, those who love violence,
he hates with a passion.
On the wicked he will rain
fiery coals and burning sulfur;
a scorching wind will be their lot.
For the Lord is righteous,
he loves justice;
the upright will see his face.

This is a very challenging text for many believers, and as we move forward it's important to build upon the understanding that the Bible is authoritative in every way. Just because I don't like how something sounds does not mean it's not true or what God's heart is. That being said, this passage makes one thing very clear to us: not only does God hate sin, but God hates sinners. Consider for a moment though that hatred in God's eyes plays out very differently from our own hatred. God is able to simultaneously hate and love something in full force. We cannot. This text is also not the only passage wherein the Bible uses this specific terminology. I would encourage you to study Ps 5:5–6, Prov 6:16–19, and Hos 9:15 as additional examples. To provide a bit of context, the word *hate* in Hebrew is *"sane"* (pronounced "saw-nay"). *"Sane"* in the Hebrew lexicon is depicted as a thorn and a seed which is understood to represent a thornbush. Essentially, the Hebrew definition of hatred is how we feel about thorn bushes: we despise them because of the pain they cause to the point that it leads to action (either by cutting down the bush or turning and going the other way). So it is with our King. His hatred toward the sinner is not passive, emotional hatred. It is active, destructive, and powerful. What I pray you will come to realize is that God's hatred is not his end goal. His hatred toward the sinner is always a catalyst to further pour out his love onto his people. As we have discussed, the cross is a perfect example of this. There is no greater act of hatred toward someone than by forsaking them and causing them to suffer one of the most brutal deaths in existence. Yet there is also no greater love that one can demonstrate than by dying on behalf of them.

Let's not miss though how God's hatred and wrath actually play out. Consider the story of Jonah for a moment. God sent Jonah to the Ninevites (who we just discussed would be a people group God hated and was wrathful toward) to preach to them in hopes of bringing them into the fold of the Lord. Not only that, but God actually rebukes Jonah for not wanting to do so out of not thinking they deserved it! Similarly, Jesus sets the precedent of dining with (but not being yoked with) sinners, who would also be his enemies. And so, we have the wonderful and beautiful paradox of God's love and wrath. God's love is used to draw people to himself, that he may be glorified. Likewise, God's wrath is used to make his sovereignty evident to all people, that they (specifically those who are not his people) would be drawn to him and so glorify him.

The reality of the situation is that, upon reading this, you may have had different experiences that impact how you process this truth. This may be the first time you have ever heard this truth, or perhaps the Lord has not revealed its significance to you, or it may be that, as of now, you refuse to believe it. That is completely okay. While you were once the object of both God's love and wrath, if you are truly born again, then even though certain things are still a mystery to you, you live under God's love alone. There is an invitation here to lean into the aspects of God's character that may not have been revealed to us yet. Part of the beauty of sanctification is in God's continual unveiling of his own truths in order "*to work out your salvation with fear and trembling*" (Phil 2:12) by processing with the Lord. I whole-heartedly trust the

Spirit to intercede in this area if you remain in submission to him and trust God's word.

1 THESSALONIANS 5:9-10

> *For God did not appoint us to suffer wrath but to receive salvation through our Lord Jesus Christ. He died for us so that, whether we are awake or asleep, we may live together with him.*

The beauty within God's hatred is that he doesn't want us to remain within it. His heart is to bring us into a right relationship with him. This is where the cross becomes so awesome to us. God was not content with us being under his wrath, so "*through our Lord Jesus Christ,*" we are brought into the family. Take for example two laser pointers shining directly at you. One laser represents God's love, while the other represents his wrath. Both are being given to you in full effect and at all times. Now picture Jesus stepping in front of the laser pointer representing wrath. What happens? The entirety of the wrath laser is intercepted by Jesus and all that remains on you is the love laser. This is a picture of how it functions for us when we are saved by the cross of Christ. The fullness of God's wrath is given to Jesus so that all that we experience is the Father's love. His hatred and wrath toward our sin is not lessened, it is fully seized by the cross.

MALACHI 1:2-3

> "*I have loved you,*" *says the Lord.*
>   "*But you ask, 'How have you loved us?'*
>   "*Was not Esau Jacob's brother?*" *declares the Lord.*
> "*Yet I have loved Jacob, but Esau I have hated, and I have turned his hill country into a wasteland and left his inheritance to the desert jackals.*"

Not only does God remove the hatred and wrath from those that are his people, but he also uses his wrath as a way for us to see his love more evidently. The Lord responds to the Israelites' question of "*how have you loved us?*" by framing his love for them around his hatred for Esau (who had sinned against him). So, we as believers are able to rejoice in this beautiful progression God provides for us: God hated us because of our sin, yet he yearned to show us mercy, so he gave us the cross, enabling us to see his love more radiantly through the wrath that is still being poured out onto his enemies. The more we are able to grow in our understanding of God's hatred, anger, and wrath toward us apart from Christ, the more tremendous in size the cross becomes. When I see how large the debt is that I owed, the one who paid the debt becomes ever sweeter to me. If I allow myself to accept the fact that I truly was the man on death row, saved when I was in desperate need, my gratitude toward my Savior grows exponentially.

Chapter Five

The Unique and Specific Love

Whoever has my commands and keeps them is the one who loves me. The one who loves me will be loved by my Father, and I too will love them and show myself to them.

—JOHN 14:21

The Lord confides in those who fear him; he makes his covenant known to them. My eyes are ever on the Lord, for only he will release my feet from the snare.

—PSALM 25:14–15

IT IS IMPORTANT TO take a bit of a detour and acknowledge what many may be thinking: What about the unbeliever? Are they just left out in the dust? I thought God loved all people equally? While I cannot speak to if the magnitude of God's love toward believers and unbelievers is equivalent, what I can confidently say, backed by God's word, is that it manifests itself in drastically different ways.

Reformed theology uses the terms *common grace* and *special grace* to lay the groundwork for this understanding. Common grace would be any grace that God gives out to all people, regardless of whether or not they are born again. Common grace is what enables people to breathe air, enjoy a sunset, or even not drop dead when they sin. These graces are the things in life that all people naturally encounter because of God's love. In contrast, special grace is the specific grace given to believers that is unique and cannot be received by unbelievers. A couple examples of this would be receiving salvation by way of Jesus's blood or being enlightened in your spiritual giftings.

If we spend any amount of time studying God's character throughout the Bible, one thing becomes abundantly clear: God adores his people and will do whatever it takes to everyone else in order to enable them to experience his love and provision. This does not mean that God does not love those who are not his people, but as we spoke about in the previous chapter, the reality of the situation is that he also hates them. We as believers experience exclusively his love and are connected to him by way of the cross in a way that unbelievers could never experience without salvation.

One way that we as people tend to really fall short in interpreting God's word in this area is by foregoing context for the sake of application. It's incredibly easy to throw a verse at someone to try to comfort them, even if it contextually does not apply. Or we may even pick a text out of the Bible to lift ourselves up when we are feeling down without knowing who or what the Scripture was written for. There are a countless number of beautiful, tenderhearted, and encouraging verses about God's love, but almost all of them are directed to *his* people alone. Much of the time it is alongside verses about God pouring out his wrath onto enemies for the sake of his people. Take for a moment one of the most popular verses of our time, Zeph 3:17:

> The Lord your God is with you,
> the Mighty Warrior who saves.
> he will take great delight in you;
> in his love he will no longer rebuke you,
> but will rejoice over you with singing.

If this verse doesn't encourage you of God's heart toward you, then I don't know what will! We can't miss who this is written to, though. All of Zeph 3 is written to the Israelites, who were God's chosen people. This verse is not meant to display general love given to all people, but a very specific love toward his unique, exclusive people at the expense of everyone else. And as God is unchanging, we know that this unique love over the Israelites is identical to his unique love for us as his children here and now. We see proof of this disparity of love just a few verses earlier in verse 8:

> *"Therefore wait for me,"*
> *declares the Lord,*
> *"for the day I will stand up to testify.*
> *I have decided to assemble the nations,*
> *to gather the kingdoms*
> *and to pour out my wrath on them—*
> *all my fierce anger.*
> *The whole world will be consumed*
> *by the fire of my jealous anger."*

When we generalize verses to comfort either ourselves or someone else, we do nothing other than cause damage. Misusing God's word in such a way as this confirms a lie that many people believe: God loves all people equally. He absolutely does not love all people equally and here are just a few evidences of this:

- Noah's Ark—God, in his anger and wrath toward the wicked, wipes them from the earth, saving only a select few due to their faith (Gen 6–7).

- Moses and the Exodus—God leads the entirety of his people safely through the Red Sea and promptly drowns the entire army of Pharaoh that was chasing them (Exod 14).

- David and Goliath—God uses his chosen follower, David, to single-handedly win the fight against the Philistines, who were not believers (1 Sam 17).

- The Judgment Seat—Only those who are God's beloved will enter into eternal rest with him, and those who are not will experience eternity away from him in torment (Rev 20).

This is some serious stuff that we have to work to understand if we hope to see God's character without blur. God goes to many lengths to show his unique love for his children, and it wearies the Lord when we squander it by acting as if all are under this love:

> *You have wearied the Lord with your words.*
> *"How have we wearied him?" you ask.*
> *By saying, "All who do evil are good in the eyes of the*
> *Lord, and he is pleased with them" or "Where is the God of*
> *justice?"* (Mal 2:17)

Let's not miss this. Let's not act like common grace to all is equivalent to special grace to the redeemed. You, believer, are so uniquely loved by the King and he wants you to understand the depth of his love for you. Does his distinct love for you lessen his love for the lost? By no means! In fact, his unique and covenantal love was always used with the agenda of bringing the nations to himself by provoking the unbeliever to want to know him, as proven through the story of Jonah we discussed in chapter 4. If this is something you struggle to believe, I encourage you to pray into Matt 18:12–14 to see God's abundant love for the lost sheep.

Nonetheless, every nonbeliever is at the mercy of the King's sovereignty, especially when it comes to him displaying his heart for you, his beloved. Allow this to sweeten the fragrance of God's love. Enable it to grow your heart for the lost and propel you further into ministry, understanding what is at stake and what the unsaved are missing out on. Understanding God's unique love for you opens the door to increasing the size of the cross in your life. We can see more clearly what we were saved from and brought into. Take a moment to simply ponder how you were once *"wretched, pitiful, poor, blind and naked"* (Rev 3:17) but are now *"whiter than snow"* (Ps 51:7). Oh, how wonderful the cross becomes when we see how wide the gap was that our Father crossed to be with us. What a gift Jesus is to the redeemed!

Chapter Six

The Heart of Ambivalent Gratitude

It was good for me to be afflicted so that I might learn your decrees.

—Psalm 119:71

Now I, Nebuchadnezzar, praise and exalt and glorify the King of heaven, because everything he does is right and all his ways are just. And those who walk in pride he is able to humble.

—Daniel 4:37

IF YOU'RE UNFAMILIAR WITH the story arc surrounding King Nebuchadnezzar, let me fill you in. Nebuchadnezzar was king during the first few chapters of the book of Daniel as well as many other places in scripture. In short, he was a really rotten guy. You may have heard of the story regarding Shadrach, Meshach, and Abednego being thrown into the furnace for not worshiping a statue that the king had built in Dan 3. That was this king. After God saved them from the flames, Nebuchadnezzar had a "change of heart." I put this in quotes because he decided that instead of burning people for not worshiping his idol, he would just chop them up into pieces if they *say anything against the God of Shadrach, Meshach and Abednego*" (Dan 3:29). Not exactly God honoring, but I guess it's an attempt.

Where the story gets really fascinating, in my opinion, is in chapter 4. After Daniel had interpreted a dream for him, Nebuchadnezzar still hadn't learned his lesson. During a stroll on the roof of his palace, he said *"Is not this the great Babylon I have built as the royal residence, by my mighty power and for the glory of my majesty?"* (Dan 4:30). Immediately after saying this, a heavenly voice told him that he would lose everything he had, be like a wild animal, and be cast into the wilderness for a time. And so it was for King Nebuchadnezzar. It would be a normal tendency (albeit unjust) for anyone to be drawn into bitterness toward God if this happened to them. I mean, what would I do if I experienced bodily abnormalities, feral tendencies, and the loss of everything I had because of God's power? But this king had a very different response, as we see in Dan 4:34–37:

> At the end of that time, I, Nebuchadnezzar, raised my eyes toward heaven, and my sanity was restored. Then I praised the Most High; I honored and glorified him who lives forever.
>
> His dominion is an eternal dominion;
> his kingdom endures from generation to generation.
> All the peoples of the earth
> are regarded as nothing.
> He does as he pleases
> with the powers of heaven
> and the peoples of the earth.
> No one can hold back his hand
> or say to him: "What have you done?"
>
> At the same time that my sanity was restored, my honor and splendor were returned to me for the glory of my kingdom. My advisers and nobles sought me out, and

I was restored to my throne and became even greater than before. Now I, Nebuchadnezzar, praise and exalt and glorify the King of heaven, because everything he does is right and all his ways are just. And those who walk in pride he is able to humble.

Wait, so this man, after having his entire life wrecked by God, turns toward Heaven and praises his name? I find that absolutely wild! If we could adopt even a sliver of this mindset, our whole world would be transformed. All throughout our lives we will encounter difficult circumstances, and there typically will be three possible reactions we can display:

1. Anger and indignation toward the Lord or the situation in which we blame him as if he wronged us.

2. Disregard for the Lord in which we fail to acknowledge his existence in the situation.

3. Turning to the Lord out of reverence and praising him in the midst of hardship.

What I want to propose to you is that you will not find a benefit within the first two types of reactions (outside of God using our reaction to further glorify himself), but you will always benefit from engaging in the third type of reaction. There are a seemingly endless amount of biblical texts calling us to praise the Lord during difficulties. Here are just a few in addition to the model that Nebuchadnezzar gives us:

David, when running for his life from Saul, writes in Ps 34:1–3, "*I will extol the Lord at all times; his praise will always be on my lips. I will glory in the Lord; let the afflicted hear and rejoice. Glorify the Lord with me; let us exalt his name together.*"

Habakkuk, during troublesome and stressful times, prays in Hab 3:17–19, "*Though the fig tree does not bud and there are no grapes on the vines, though the olive crop fails and the fields produce no food, though there are no sheep in the pen and no cattle in the stalls, yet I will rejoice in the Lord, I will be joyful in God my Savior. The Sovereign Lord is my strength; he makes my feet like the feet of a deer, he enables me to tread on the heights.*"

James begins his letter to the tribes of Israel with a strong call in Jas 1:2–3 to "*consider it pure joy, my brothers and sisters, whenever you face trials of many kinds, because you know that the testing of your faith produces perseverance.*"

We see that these examples lead us to an understanding that, no matter what happens to us, we should always look to God with exaltation and worship. When we lean into this area of worship, though, it's important to understand both the "why" and "how" regarding praise despite circumstance. The journey to understanding the answer to these two questions will open the doorway to a new way of living: the way God yearns for us to live.

Before we dive in, I want to take a moment to acknowledge that painful circumstances are very real and very, well, painful. By no means does a call to gratitude and joy diminish a potential need to grieve or feel pain. In fact, Ps 126:5–6 declares that "*those who sow with tears will reap with songs of joy. Those who go out weeping, carrying seed to sow, will return with songs of joy, carrying sheaves with them.*" The Bible does not act as if following the Lord will mean that we won't experience pain or grief. Rather it provides a model to encounter joy in the midst of that pain. If you are weathering a difficult life circumstance, I want to say that I am sorry. No amount of Bible verses or encouraging words can remove all the physical, emotional, and mental pain we may feel. But my hope is that through what we will be further examining, we can come to a place of smiling as we look to Heaven, even as tears stream down our faces. You *can* experience joy in the midst of pain. Let the Lord continue to shepherd you through this season. After all, he is the Good Shepherd.

Why should we praise God during hard times? This question is a bit easier to navigate than the latter, as the answer is the same as why we honor him during good times. We praise him simply because "*great is the Lord and most worthy of praise; his greatness no one can fathom*" (Ps 145:3). God is a great God! He deserves all the praise we can give him. As we discussed in chapter 1 of this book, you exist for the sole purpose of lifting his name high, and in turn you will experience maximized joy. Your purpose doesn't change just because there happens to be a rain cloud above your life at a certain moment or a valley that takes many years to walk through. The reality of the situation is that God has redeemed suffering. Many scriptures examine the joys of suffering, but consider Phil 3:7–11:

> *But whatever were gains to me I now consider loss for the sake of Christ. What is more, I consider everything a loss because of the surpassing worth of knowing Christ Jesus my Lord, for whose sake I have lost all things. I consider them garbage, that I may gain Christ and be found in him, not having a righteousness of my own that comes from the law, but that which is through faith in Christ—the righteousness that comes from God on the basis of faith. I want to know Christ—yes, to know the power of his resurrection and participation in his sufferings, becoming like him in his death, and so, somehow, attaining to the resurrection from the dead.*

Paul is actually excited about the prospect of participating in the sufferings of Christ because this suffering will allow him to become more like Christ whether in life or in death. Jesus dying for you, conquering death for you, and providing the Holy Spirit to you has made any amount of suffering a redeemed event. Paul takes it all a step further in Rom 8 when in verse 18 he considers *"that our present sufferings are not worth comparing with the glory that will be revealed in us."* I love the quote by the 1600s poet George Herbert, that claims "Death used to be an executioner, but the gospel has made him just a gardener." Because of what Jesus accomplished on the cross, death simply plants us so that we can grow into who we were originally intended to be: a beloved son or daughter in perfect harmony with our king for eternity. So, why should we praise God during hard times? Because all suffering, even unto death, will bring us closer to Jesus, the source of joy.

The *why* becomes ever more potent when we acknowledge our wretchedness and deserved death on top of God's greatness. I should praise him because no matter how bad things get, I will always deserve immeasurably worse. To be clear, sin does bring about pain and suffering, but general suffering in life is not punishment for your or anyone else's sins but rather is a vehicle that God is using to bring glory to his name and joy to his people (see John 9:1–12 for evidence of this reality). God saved me from the worst circumstance of all (eternity apart from him), and therefore I should glorify him every second of every day. Does all of this mean that it will always be a walk in the park to praise his name during tribulation? Absolutely not. The Bible never says this will be easy, but it makes it abundantly clear that this is necessary.

How do we praise God during hard times? This question is a bit trickier to answer because we first have to believe the answer to *why* we praise God. If I don't believe to my core that the Lord deserves praise at all times, then I won't ever feel led to worship within hardship and pain. But if I believe that I am by nature a wretch, deserving of nothing but the worst possible outcome (without drifting into the pride of thinking too low of myself), I am able to come before him with my "how": ambivalent gratitude. Ambivalent gratitude is the heart posture of clinging to thanksgiving, hope, and joy in the midst of pain and hardship that works to bring us down even though the world and our flesh may tell us not to. It looks like experiencing mixed feelings and emotions as your heart breaks for the situation while singing with joy to the Lord. David understood this when he explained in Ps 103:10–11 that "*[the Lord] does not treat us as our sins deserve or repay us according to our iniquities. For as high as the heavens are above the earth, so great is his love for those who fear him*" and also in Ps 69:29–30 by crying out, "*I am in pain and distress; may your salvation, O God, protect me. I will praise God's name in song and glorify him with thanksgiving.*" No matter what I encounter, it will never be the worst possible outcome, meaning that I can be grateful within the pain. Therefore, no matter what form of lemons life may bring, we can always be grateful that they weren't rotten. The more we can press into having a heart of ambivalent gratitude when things aren't going our way, the more we will be able encounter joy in the midst of it all. In fact, Paul takes it even further by saying that we should *glory* in our suffering in Rom 5:1–5:

> *Therefore, since we have been justified through faith, we have peace with God through our Lord Jesus Christ, through whom we have gained access by faith into this grace in which we now stand. And we boast in the hope of the glory of God. Not only so, but we also glory in our sufferings, because we know that suffering produces perseverance; perseverance, character; and character, hope. And hope does not put us to shame, because God's love has been poured out into our hearts through the Holy Spirit, who has been given to us.*

Let's make this more personal for us. Many of us have either battled cancer ourselves or known someone who is or was battling cancer. I will never forget the day that my parents invited my brother, sister, and I to a seemingly normal meal at Mimi's Cafe. It was there that my mom explained to us that she had been diagnosed with throat cancer. It was March of 2018, and I was a junior in college at the time. By nature, my family was confronted with the need to respond. The response, as we discussed earlier, would either be anger, disregard, or praise. While, by the grace of God, my mom was cured after undergoing surgery, I still look back and wish I had stepped into that difficult time with more of a heart of gratitude. How much more intimate of a time could it have been with the Lord if I praised him for what he was doing in that moment. Do I deserve a mom? No. Do I deserve a mom that has sacrificed so much and loved me so well throughout my life? Of course not. Do I deserve to have a mom that lives long enough to see my own children grow up? Again, I do not. This is where we come to the crossroads of ambivalent gratitude and indignation. My mom had cancer and I had the choice to be grateful for what the Lord was doing in that space or indignant that he let her get sick. If my mom had passed away from the cancer, I would have had the choice to be grateful for the mother that God gave me when I didn't deserve it or indignant that she was taken away.

Now, I know we are getting very real, very fast, but this is vital for us to grasp in our pursuit of the King. Will I choose to engage in the reality that the God of the hills is the same God of the valleys? Or will I miss out on this large portion of my walk with him? It's okay if this takes time for you to process or if it even brings about emotion. I wholeheartedly trust the Lord to grow in you this truth that he has grown me in. You see, this choice between gratitude and indignation extends to any difficult situation in life. If I lose my job, will I be grateful that God blessed me with a job in the first place when I didn't deserve it, or will I be indignant that he threw a hardship at me? If I lose my arm in an accident, will I be grateful that God allowed me to keep one arm when I don't deserve any, or will I be indignant that he crippled me? And very importantly, if God seemingly doesn't answer my prayer, will I be grateful that his way is right and that he has given me access to talk to him, or will I be indignant that he seemingly didn't listen to me or help me the way I wanted him to? We have to fight our sinful urges to be entitled in this area. I am not entitled to *anything* good in this life. Everything that is less terrible than the worst possible outcome is a gift and a showing of God's grace. Not only do we not deserve anything good, but the Bible actually makes it clear that I have no right to be angry at God for what he allows to happen. Let's look at two very clear pictures that God gives us regarding people being angry at God out of ignorance: Job and Jonah.

In the first two chapters of Job's book, he loses his cattle and servants to raiders and fire, his children are killed from a collapsed building, he is afflicted with painful sores from head to toe, and his wife tempts him to "*curse God and die*" (2:9). The crazy thing about all of this is that it is by God's authority that it happens. After a few dozen chapters go by in which Job and his friends sit around being upset with God and questioning his love, God spends chapters 38 to 41 calling them out for their foolishness. God makes it very clear that they are ignorant in their accusations when he asks in Job 38:2, "*Who is this that obscures my plans with words without knowledge?*" After Job realizes what he has done, he turns toward God with greater understanding and says in Job 42:2–6:

> *I know that you can do all things;*
> *no purpose of yours can be thwarted.*
> *You asked, "Who is this that obscures my plans without knowledge?"*
> *Surely I spoke of things I did not understand,*

things too wonderful for me to know.
You said, "Listen now, and I will speak;
I will question you,
and you shall answer me."
My ears had heard of you
but now my eyes have seen you.
Therefore I despise myself
and repent in dust and ashes.

After all is said and done, Job repents of being angry at God and considers what happened to him as "wonderful." None of Job's response makes sense unless we fully grasp the reality that God allowed these things to happen to Job out of his goodness and love and that Job is wrong for questioning God's character in it.

In a similar vein, Jonah's story (which we touched on earlier) is about feeling as though he was mistreated by God. You may be familiar with the part of the story where Jonah is swallowed by a huge fish (modern media tends to portray it as a whale). This is because God told Jonah to preach truth to the Ninevites and Jonah ran away since he didn't think the Ninevites deserved to be saved. After a final confrontation with God in the book of Jonah chapter 4, we see two evidences of Jonah's lack of understanding of God's love and his own deservedness:

1. Jonah explains why he ran away and that he didn't want God to save the people of Nineveh. God then responds in verse 4 with *"is it right for you to be angry?"*

2. God provides a plant to give Jonah shade while he waits to see what God will do. After a day, God sends a worm to eat the plant so that it no longer blocks the sun, and Jonah becomes upset by the scorching heat. God then responds in verse 9 with *"is it right for you to be angry about the plant?"*

What Jonah had failed to understand is that all things are under God's reign, and he is right and just in doing whatever he pleases, because no matter what he does, it is good. Jonah felt that he deserved better than what he was dealt, but God graciously puts him in his place at the very end of the book by saying:

*You have been concerned about this plant, though you did
not tend it or make it grow. It sprang up overnight and died
overnight. And should I not have concern for the great city
of Nineveh, in which there are more than a hundred and
twenty thousand people who cannot tell their right hand
from their left—and also many animals?* (Jonah 4:10–11)

Who are we to think that we know better than God? He is love
incarnate *"and we know that in all things God works for the good of
those who love him, who have been called according to his purpose"*
(Rom 8:28). If I fall into the trap of anger and dissatisfaction, I will
never be able to fully see and believe his goodness in every situation. But if I allow him to grow my heart into encountering gratitude no matter if I experience the highest of highs or the lowest of
lows, then I will bring more glory to his name and will undergo joy
like no other. This is how, as we have already seen, Paul is able to
declare in Rom 8:18 *"I consider that our present sufferings are not
worth comparing with the glory that will be revealed in us."*

How does a heart of ambivalent gratitude magnify the cross
in our lives? It is a daily surrender of our worldly lives and a humble acceptance of all that Jesus is and calls us into. When we choose
to be thankful, though the world would say we don't have reason
to be, we concurrently acknowledge that Christ on the cross saved
us from what we naturally deserve apart from him. Thank you, Father, for choosing to shift your wrath off of me and onto your Son,
that I may look upon you in the midst of the storm with gratitude.
For no matter how much the wind and the waves toss me about, it
will never compare to the price that was paid on my behalf.

I believe that a sticking point in all I have written will be understanding God's goodness. What if we do not see what God is doing
as inherently "good"? How do we come before him with gratitude?
Let's take some time to look closer at God's good character and potentially see where our definition of "good" has gone awry.

Chapter Seven

The Foundational Goodness

Taste and see that the Lord is good; blessed is the one who takes refuge in him.

—PSALM 34:8

You are good, and what you do is good; teach me your decrees.

—PSALM 119:68

IF YOU DO A quick internet search of the definition of the word *good* you will see that the internet defines it as "that which is morally right." The issue with this particular word is that it's entirely subjective based upon the beholder's moral compass. Everyone on the planet views something as good. But what that "something" is differs drastically from person to person based on areas such as familial upbringing, learned ideologies and beliefs, life events, or even our relationships and line of work. Modern media has done much in shaping the way we view the world, but one way that I find very interesting is how we view good and evil. Most storybook villains depict some person who is wicked to their core and wants to either take over the world or watch it burn. The motive is generally something ridiculous that causes audiences to despise the villain all the more. Likewise, we tend to view "bad" people in our world as heartless beings that want nothing but to do evil and inflict pain.

The issue with generalizing people in this way is that it tends to omit the *real* person's morality. As an example, let's look at Marvel's Thanos. If you're unfamiliar, he is the chief villain in the Marvel films *Avengers: Infinity War* and *Avengers: Endgame*. I was very interested by the character development given to Thanos throughout the films as, to be honest, his motive kind of made sense. His primary goal was to fill a special gauntlet with unique stones so that he could eradicate half of the universe's life. This, on the surface, seems insane and the act of a mad scientist supervillain. But throughout the films, we see why he is doing what he's doing: to bring balance and allow planets to prosper. He saw real hardship being brought about by overpopulation and saw planets thrive by wiping out half of their inhabitants. Now, do I think that what Thanos was trying to do is morally right? Absolutely not. But it's vital to note that *he* thought his actions were morally right. He genuinely wanted to make the universe a thriving and balanced place.

Let's look at a more tangible example. Imagine how the quarterback on a primarily passing football team feels when, just before their game, a downpour of rain begins and shows no signs of letting up. This would generally be a cause for concern as throwing the football accurately becomes more difficult when your hands and the ball are soaking wet. Rain in this case is not a good thing. Now imagine the feeling a farmer down the road feels during this rainstorm after he's had a season of drought, causing his crop to struggle. He would likely be overjoyed and led to celebrate it as a gift. Rain in this case is absolutely a good thing.

How can this be? How can some things be generally agreed upon as good or bad while other things are so divisive? It's because we have it all backwards. We create within ourselves our own definitions of the word *good* and then apply it to our daily lives. Or, even worse, we allow culture to dictate our view of good and bad. It is likely apparent to you how this can get in the way of our understanding the goodness of God. We attribute our definition of goodness to God rather than allowing him, the creator and embodiment of goodness to dictate how we see it. Author and theologian C. S. Lewis once said that "God is not merely good, but goodness; goodness is not merely divine, but God."[1] What fools we are to think that we know better than God in this area. He created all things to be good, righteous, and holy, and we were the ones to go and screw it all up. Now we think we are smart enough to determine what is good and bad, right and wrong? It is absolutely nonsensical.

James 1:17 states that *"every good and perfect gift is from above, coming down from the Father of the heavenly lights, who does not change like shifting shadows."* Let's not miss one very important distinction in this verse. It does not say that *only* good gifts come from God, but that *every* good gift comes from God. Everything good in existence is of the Lord and, as we discussed in chapter 1, for the Lord. Not only is God the full embodiment of goodness, but within him exists no evil, as made clear in 1 John 1:5 when the apostle John says, *"God is light; in him there is no darkness at all."* So, what we have here is this beautiful yet challenging truth that God is perfectly *good* with no *bad* within him. Well then, if we are supposed to frame our view of goodness around God, what does it mean to be "good"?

> *Since, then, you have been raised with Christ, set your hearts on things above, where Christ is, seated at the right hand of God. Set your minds on things above, not on earthly things. For you died, and your life is now hidden with Christ in God.* (Col 3:1–3)

Paul gives us this model of what it means to be good. As James made clear that God is good and sends goodness down from above, Paul explains that engaging with these things from above is the solution. Goodness comes from above, therefore we should

---

1. Lewis, "Poison of Subjectivism," 80.

"*set our hearts on things above*." When we fully enable the goodness of God to dictate what we view as good, our mindset in the midst of trying times will be transformed. This enables me then, when my mom is diagnosed with cancer, to more readily trust that the King is working for the good of his glory and his people.

My daughter, Lauren, had to have a procedure done when she was just a few weeks old to remove class IV (most severe) lip and tongue ties because they would have caused many issues later on in her life. For three weeks following the procedure, my wife and I had to do "stretches" for her where we would pull on the lip and tongue while rubbing the wound with pressure so that the ties would not grow back. As you would imagine, Lauren was not a fan of this and would cry every time out of pain and discomfort. We could see in those moments what Lauren couldn't: the momentary hardship now would benefit her greatly down the line. To be honest, this reality is the only thing that kept us in the game of doing her stretches as it was often almost too much to bear for us to put her through the pain. Now if my wife and I, who are by nature flawed, are able to see the good in the midst of the pain, how much more so does God, who holds all things in the palm of his hands, allow the pain in our lives because he knows the good it will bring about. We truly see in part what God sees in full. We have to fight hard to resist the temptation of believing that anything can happen outside of God's inherent goodness.

I won't dive too deep into the realm of the enemy and spiritual warfare here, as this will be addressed more appropriately in a future chapter, but we need to acknowledge satan in this area. As we already noted that no evil exists within or through God, we now need to address the reality that evil is fully embodied in the person of the devil. "*The one who does what is sinful is of the devil, because the devil has been sinning from the beginning. The reason the Son of God appeared was to destroy the devil's work*" (1 John 3:8). On the one hand we have God, who exists for our good through his glory, and on the other hand we have satan, who exists to do bad. In chapter 5 we examined briefly the life of Job, but we didn't discuss how the tragedy he went through came about. In chapter 1 of the book of Job, God enables the devil to attack Job by saying *"Have you considered my servant Job? There is no one on earth like him; he is blameless and upright, a man who fears God and shuns evil"* (Job 1:8). Likewise, a similar thing happens in chapter 2 when God again enables the devil to attack Job by saying, *"Have you considered my servant Job? There is no one on earth like him; he is blameless and upright, a man who fears God and shuns evil. And he still maintains his integrity, though you incited me against him to ruin him without any reason"* (Job 2:3). What we analyzed in the later chapters of Job is that God allowed satan to do these things not outside of his goodness but *because of* his goodness. John Piper, in his sermon titled "Satan Always Asks Permission: Seven Ways God Reigns over Evil," explains well the dynamic between our Lord and our enemy:

> When satan wants to destroy a saint, he must get permission before he touches him. So, he comes to God and says, "Job only worships you because he's rich. If I take his camels, donkeys, servants, he'll curse you" (see Job 1:9–11). And God gives him permission, but he puts a limit. "Don't you touch his body" (see Job 1:12). So, he kills them all. Job falls on his face: *"The Lord gave, and the Lord has taken away"* (Job 1:21). Satan has to get permission to go after his body, and he gets it. But God says, "Don't you kill him" (see Job 2:6). Isn't that remarkable? So satan does harm to us, but not without God's say.[2]

What a beautiful truth it is to know that God has satan on a short leash. In an even more incredible fashion, God is able to use both our own and satan's depravity to bring about his goodness. Let's look at two people in the Bible that I believe highlight this well: Joseph and Jesus.

Joseph had a wild ride of a life. He was sold into slavery by his brothers out of jealousy where he was then wrongly thrown into prison for a crime he did not commit. By a miraculous turn of events, God provides Joseph with power and the opportunity to work directly underneath Pharaoh. After world events cause strife

2. Piper, "Satan Always Asks Permission."

within the nation, Joseph's brothers have to come before him (while he remained unknown to them) and ask for help. After Joseph reveals himself to his brothers and they are scared of what he may do to them because of their wrongdoings, we see Joseph respond with grace in Gen 50:19–21: *"But Joseph said to them, 'Don't be afraid. Am I in the place of God? You intended to harm me, but God intended it for good to accomplish what is now being done, the saving of many lives. So then, don't be afraid. I will provide for you and your children.' And he reassured them and spoke kindly to them."* God knew exactly what he was doing throughout the entirety of Joseph's life. If we cling to the Lord the way Joseph does, we are untouchable by man. Nothing can happen to us apart from God's perfect will. And if his will be done, we can trust that it is good.

Perhaps the most powerful example of God's sovereignty over evil, though, is found in Jesus on the cross. The enemy wanted nothing more than to kill Jesus and worked hard to do so, as we see in Luke 22:3 when *"satan entered Judas, called Iscariot, one of the Twelve."* If you're unfamiliar, Judas was originally one of the twelve disciples but decided to backstab Jesus for a little extra cash. I imagine that satan had crafted this plan that he thought would bring about his victory. He would infiltrate the ranks of the twelve disciples and use one of them to bring about the death of Jesus, the King. But as we know, the cross was actually the Lord's decisive victory over sin and death. What the enemy tried to use as a way of thwarting God's reign, God actually used to bring us closer to himself by way of a new covenant. What a miraculous reality of our God that in his embodied goodness and sovereignty, every hardship that we encounter is actually being worked for our good and his glory, no matter if we witness the fruits of it in this life or the next.

I want to close this chapter by answering the question "why." Why is it important to view God as good and to have my understanding of goodness be transformed? Well, not only are we encouraged to do so by way of Isa 5:20 when the prophet declares, *"Woe to those who call evil good, and good evil, who put darkness for light and light for darkness, who put bitter for sweet and sweet for bitter,*" but this is the final piece of the puzzle regarding chapter 5. Ambivalent gratitude, or pressing into gratitude in the midst of hardship, is only possible if we are convinced of the goodness of God. Our Lord yearns to lead us into a place of unwavering joy despite circumstance, but in order to do so we need to trust him in every aspect of our lives, no matter how difficult it may seem. This won't likely come easy nor quickly to us. This will be something we need to engage with daily until it becomes our new heartbeat. I encourage you to give it a try and see what God can do with it. When pain strikes your life, first look to God and acknowledge that he is good and working for your good. Then, acknowledge the reality of what you naturally deserve. Out of this, give thanks to God for his grace upon you within the trial. As you put this into practice, the cross will become more evident in and through you. You will bring your King more glory as you worship and praise him amid pain, and you will experience a greater joy as we receive fullness of life through Christ on the cross. Will all this make the circumstance disappear? Not likely. But you *will* likely encounter the Lord in a way you may otherwise miss and experience the joy he died to bring us.

Chapter Eight

The Road to Rome

The following night the Lord stood near Paul and said, "Take courage! As you have testified about me in Jerusalem, so you must also testify in Rome."

—Acts 23:11

In the previous chapters we've discussed a few instances where God's goodness and sovereignty transcended what we may have deemed "bad." One specific story arc that we haven't yet touched on is what I like to call Paul's "road to Rome" experience. The Lord led Paul through various wild and difficult occurrences in order to bring him to Rome. We oftentimes settle into God's work within the beginning and end of Paul's narrative (road to Damascus and the Epistles) without acknowledging the beauty of the in-between. That being said, let's take some time to really engage with Paul's journey, as the more we understand the path God laid out for him, the easier it will become to accept our own "road to Rome" experiences, regardless of what they may look like.

For some context, after Paul encountered the Lord on the road to Damascus, he was spurred on to preach the good news of Jesus to the world, which is exactly what he began doing. He went from town to town, weathering immense tribulation, boldly proclaiming Jesus as the one true King. While Paul did make multiple trips to Jerusalem, his final journey there in Acts 21 is what propels him into deeper waters. The disciples in Tyre were led by the Spirit to foresee this as *"through the Spirit they urged Paul not to go on to Jerusalem"* (Acts 21:4). After another round of attempted dissuasion from the disciples while in Caesarea, Paul finally responds by saying in Acts 21:13, *"Why are you weeping and breaking my heart? I am ready not only to be bound, but also to die in Jerusalem for the name of the Lord Jesus."* It didn't matter what people said. Paul was confident of where the Lord was leading him, and he wasn't going to let anything stand in the way of his God-given convictions.

In Jerusalem, Paul very quickly stirred the pot by speaking the truth of Christ. He was arrested, flogged, and brought before the Sanhedrin (a group of religious elites) to make an appeal. After Paul was forcibly removed from the Sanhedrin due to fears that he would be killed, he was given his final mission: *"The following night the Lord stood near Paul and said, 'Take courage! As you have testified about me in Jerusalem, so you must also testify in Rome'"* (Acts 23:11). As we investigate deeper into Paul's calling, it will benefit us to look into two specific areas of focus within the story: the means and the submission.

The Means

> *Many are the plans in a person's heart, but it is the Lord's purpose that prevails.* (Prov 19:21).
> *There is no wisdom, no insight, no plan that can succeed against the Lord.* (Prov 21:30).

How frequently do we, in our sin, fall into the trap of thinking our way is better than God's way? Whether it's because of impatience, pride, or another sin pattern, when we try to stand in the way of

God's will, it's as if we were to stand in front of a tsunami, arms stretched wide, attempting to stop its advance. It's foolish and utterly futile. God wrote the book of our lives, and each morning we simply turn the page to unveil the new mercies for the new day. Whether or not we are naturally fond of what God has in store for us on any given day is negligible, as ultimately his plan will always come to fruition. As we will soon see, God, in his grace and because of an indwelling of the Spirit, absolutely does provide to us liberties and autonomy in our pursuit of himself, but we cannot deny his sovereignty within it all. Thankfully, the more we come into an understanding of who he is, the more his plan seems delightful to us regardless of where it takes us.

What if Harry Potter decided that he didn't like how J. K. Rowling wrote the events of his life? What if he decided he didn't want to be a wizard and instead wanted to lead a simple, more normal life? Is he able to break the fourth wall, reach out of the page, and rewrite the story laid out before him? Of course not. He is bound to the will of the author, and so are we. And praise God that he executes his divine will over our lives, as he truly will provide us with the path that brings about the most joy in the end. As I've heard it said: "We see in part what God sees in full." We may not like what happens in year twenty of our lives, but could it be that God is using that season as a stepping stone to enhance our joy in him come year thirty? Again, this is all with the caveat that we aren't just some characters within God's book but rather the objects of his perfect love and therefore are given freedom to pursue him, guided by the Spirit that dwells in us. There is a balance here that we will likely not fully realize until we see the Lord face to face. But if I truly understand God as the person he is, I will gladly submit to wherever he leads me.

In Acts 5, after Peter and the other apostles stand their ground against the Sanhedrin, the Sanhedrin wanted to put them to death. In spite of this, a Pharisee named Gamaliel understood the unstoppable force that is our King when he addresses the rest of the group in Acts 5:35–39:

Men of Israel, consider carefully what you intend to do to these men. Some time ago Theudas appeared, claiming to be somebody, and about four hundred men rallied to him. He was killed, all his followers were dispersed, and it all came to nothing. After him, Judas the Galilean appeared in the days of the census and led a band of people in revolt. He too was killed, and all his followers were scattered. Therefore, in the present case I advise you: Leave these men alone! Let them go! For if their purpose or activity is of human origin, it will fail. But if it is from God, you will not be able to stop these men; you will only find yourselves fighting against God.

Praise God for being sovereign and the deciding factor in what happens to us! What a gift this was to Paul when it came to the means by which the Lord brought him to Rome. While the texts that we have surrounding Paul's journey to Rome are limited, this is at least what we know he dealt with to get there:

- In Jerusalem, after concerns that he would be ripped to pieces by an angry mob, he was housed in the Roman barracks, surrounded by soldiers to protect him. This is where he received the call to testify in Rome.

- Paul's nephew catches wind of a plot to kill Paul by more than forty men and tells the Roman commander. The commander then "*called two of his centurions and ordered them, 'Get ready a detachment of two hundred soldiers, seventy horsemen and two hundred spearmen to go to Caesarea at nine tonight. Provide horses for Paul so that he may be taken safely to Governor Felix*'" (Acts 23:23–24). Keep in mind that Caesarea was the Roman political capital in the province of Judea.

- Paul then stands trial before multiple kings and officials and he appeals to Caesar, sealing his fate to be judged by the Roman emperor himself.

- He is then shipwrecked as a prisoner on the island of Malta due to a terrible storm. From here he made his way to Rome where "*Paul was allowed to live by himself, with a soldier to guard him*" (Acts 28:16).

- For the following two years, Paul spent time preaching the good news of Jesus while under Roman guard.

Why did we take the time to go through the journey of Paul? The details are powerful and where we truly see how unbelievably miraculous God's power is. God essentially had a battalion of Roman soldiers escort Paul safely to Rome where he was able to preach God's word while still being under Roman protection. God told Paul he would testify in Rome and then used Rome's own soldiers to get him there. I find this even comical as God proves how powerless Rome, one of the most powerful nations to ever exist, is when stacked against his sovereignty. Who else could orchestrate something such as this other than God? This was Paul's "road to Rome" experience.

It is important to note that even under God's calling and provision, things were not always happy go lucky for Paul. While yes, his "road to Rome" was covered by protection, it also consisted of being beaten, threatened, shipwrecked, snake-bitten, and more. This made Paul's role in this all the more prevalent through his submission.

THE SUBMISSION

> And now, compelled by the Spirit, I am going to Jerusalem, not knowing what will happen to me there. I only know that in every city the Holy Spirit warns me that prison and hardships are facing me. However, I consider my life worth nothing to me; my only aim is to finish the race and complete the task the Lord Jesus has given me—the task of testifying to the good news of God's grace. (Acts 20:22–24)

If God called you to drop everything right now and move across the world to preach the gospel, would you go? Maybe you would go through a season of refusal? Maybe you would delay as you try to plan it all out to make sure it will go smoothly? Better yet, maybe you go without hesitation, in full submission to the Lord? There were an infinite number of ways Paul could have reacted to the urges of the Spirit, calling him into deeper waters, but how does he choose to react? In submission. Why is it so vital for us to submit to God's will the way that Paul did? There are two primary reasons: we are heard, and we are led.

> *During the days of Jesus' life on earth, he offered up prayers and petitions with fervent cries and tears to the one who could save him from death, and he was heard because of his reverent submission. Son though he was, he learned obedience from what he suffered.* (Heb 5:7–8)

Although Jesus was himself God, he still willingly modeled perfect submission to the will of the Father. As Hebrews just showed, it was out of his submission that he was heard. There is such power in giving up our strength and putting our lives into God's hands. The more we engage with this reality, the more readily we are able to sit before our Father and pour our heart out to him. As Paul lays out in Phil 2:13, *"it is God who works in you to will and to act in order to fulfill his good purpose."* The more we submit to our King, the more our thoughts and desires become like his. This is proven again in 1 John 5:14–15 when John explains that *"this is the confidence we have in approaching God: that if we ask anything according to his will, he hears us. And if we know that he hears us—whatever we ask—we know that we have what we asked of him."* Let's not miss this. We can gain assurance in our prayer life only when we submit to the sovereignty of the Lord.

> *Trust in the Lord with all your heart*
> *and lean not on your own understanding;*
> *in all your ways submit to him,*
> *and he will make your paths straight.* (Prov 3:5–6)

Not only do we have access to be heard through submission, but it also provides the space for God to lay down the brick for us to walk along. The freedom we experience in this area when we submit to God is astounding. Just imagine being able to walk through life in pure faith, trusting that every step has been dictated by the King who desires for you to have full joy. This demolishes any worries we have about what lies ahead, as our futures are made secure by the Creator of our days.

This was the key to Paul being able to willingly step into a season that he knew would bring him hardship. He trusted that the only way to encounter fullness of life is through maximizing his glorification of the Lord, which happens only through submission to him. Paul understood that the more he could get out of God's way and let him work, the better it would be for him. It is because of Paul's submission to the Lord that he is able to boldly declare in Rom 5:3–5 *"Not only so, but we also glory in our sufferings, because we know that suffering produces perseverance; perseverance, character; and character, hope. And hope does not put us to shame, because God's love has been poured out into our hearts through the Holy Spirit, who has been given to us."* The key to unwavering peace in the midst of uncertainty and hardship is found in laying down our very being before the Lord and allowing him to take full control of our lives.

Let's be diligent about how we approach our own "road to Rome" experiences. Now, our journeys will likely look very different to Paul's in practicality, but just as God knew exactly what he was doing when it came to Paul's wild ride of a life, he also knows what he is doing in yours. This holds so much power within us when we combine submission to God's will along with ambivalent gratitude. When life seemingly turns the wrong corner and puts you in a difficult situation, you have the chance to lay down your pride and entitlement, extend gratitude to the Father for his abundance of grace, and submit to all that he has in store for you, trusting that *"those who hope in the Lord will renew their strength. They will soar on wings like eagles; they will run and not grow weary, they will walk and not be faint"* (Isa 40:31).

When we choose to surrender to the path God has chosen for us, the beauty of the cross grows with each passing moment. When we say "take me wherever you will, Lord" we make known to ourselves and the rest of the world that our King deserves all the glory and every ounce of ourselves that we can give to him. Therefore, brothers and sisters, let us take heart! There is much joy to be had for us if we would allow God to take the helm of our ship. We have an intercessor, the Holy Spirit, who yearns to bring you into the joy of the Father's sovereign will. Give him the authority to take you wherever he desires. Whether the journey takes you down a road to Rome or elsewhere, it is then that we can pray like David in Ps 30:

> *I will exalt you, Lord,*
> *for you lifted me out of the depths*
> *and did not let my enemies gloat over me.*
> *Lord my God, I called to you for help,*
> *and you healed me.*
> *You, Lord, brought me up from the realm of the dead;*
> *you spared me from going down to the pit.*
> *Sing the praises of the Lord, you his faithful people;*
> *praise his holy name.*
> *For his anger lasts only a moment,*
> *but his favor lasts a lifetime;*
> *weeping may stay for the night,*
> *but rejoicing comes in the morning.*

Chapter Nine

The Exclusive Body

Consequently, you are no longer foreigners and strangers,
but fellow citizens with God's people and also members of his
household, built on the foundation of the apostles and prophets,
with Christ Jesus himself as the chief cornerstone.

—EPHESIANS 2:19–20

THE THOUGHT OF ATTEMPTING to be grateful when life turns grim and submitting to the authority of God's will despite the destination all while seeing ourselves as hell-bound wretches saved by grace can be incredibly daunting when sought after alone. That's why God has so graciously given us a community, the body of Christ, to lock arms with through the ebbs and flows of life. The issue arises when we dilute this community into being more inclusive than it was designed to be. I feel confident that this section of the book may be difficult for people, even many seasoned Christians, in today's society to receive. All around us people are pressing harder to make everything as inclusive as possible so as to not offend anyone. We live in a world of people that walk on egg-shells, scared of being canceled by the masses for saying something "wrong." Unfortunately, this inclusivity mindset has seeped into the church and has belittled the importance of something God meant for us to hold sacred: the exclusivity of the body of Christ.

Let's take a look at the book of Acts where the body came together for the first time, linked by the Holy Spirit:

> *They devoted themselves to the apostles' teaching and to fellowship, to the breaking of bread and to prayer. Every-one was filled with awe at the many wonders and signs performed by the apostles. All the believers were together and had everything in common. They sold property and possessions to give to anyone who had need. Every day they continued to meet together in the temple courts. They broke bread in their homes and ate together with glad and sincere hearts, praising God and enjoying the favor of all the people. And the Lord added to their number daily those who were being saved.* (Acts 2:42–47)

And again:

> *All the believers were one in heart and mind. No one claimed that any of their possessions was their own, but they shared everything they had.* (Acts 4:32)

I can only imagine the amount of Christ-glorification and believer-edification that came from the early church community. A group of sold-out believers, sharing everything together, praying for one another daily, and being "*one in heart and mind.*" There's no wonder God grew the number of believers so rapidly when the body of Christ was engaging in this way. As we will see, the be-lievers took this incredibly seriously to the point that anyone who was not living up to the standard that Christ calls us to was not welcome to be a part of the community any longer.

We already touched on the difference between believers and nonbelievers when it comes to God's love and wrath, but now it's important to look at how we as people experience this in real time. To a degree, the necessary exclusivity will likely make sense to most people who believe in Jesus. We understand at a foundational level that there is a clear distinction between being saved by grace and being of the world. We don't really argue with Jesus when he instructs us in Matt 7:13–14 to *"enter through the narrow gate. For wide is the gate and broad is the road that leads to destruction, and many enter through it. But small is the gate and narrow the road that leads to life, and only a few find it."* But in practicality, we are quick to act as though anyone who wants to join our church community is welcomed as a part of the body. There is a great cost to surrendering to Jesus, and a person's faith that extends only to their title (being a "Christian") just doesn't cut it in the eyes of the Lord. As we move forward in this discussion, impress onto your heart that the exclusivity of the body of Christ is never meant to hinder our pursuit of unsaved people, but rather enhance it. Don't be someone who cowers behind the body of Christ as a means of not engaging with God's heart for the lost. Your endeavors would be heavily rebuked by the word of God.

The Acts church was founded on an understanding that you were not a part of the body unless you were a dedicated follower of Jesus without any unrepentant sin existing within you. That is why Paul writes to the Corinthian church in 2 Cor 6:14, *"Do not be yoked together with unbelievers. For what do righteousness and wickedness have in common? Or what fellowship can light have with darkness?"* So where did it all go wrong? How have we fallen into this place of biblical community that is yoked so heavily with those who are not the redeemed of the Lord?

Well, primarily it comes from a place of people not actually holding the Bible as authoritative over their own thoughts, opinions, or feelings. This plays out in a few various ways:

1. We transform the "Great Commission" that Jesus gives to us in Matt 28:18–20 to read something like "therefore go and make *converts* of all nations" rather than the actual "therefore go and make *disciples* of all nations." We spend more resources extending our reach rather than growing in depth.

2. We care more about what people would think if we actually upheld the Bible than what God thinks or calls us to. We are

so afraid of being shunned, ridiculed, or cast out that we shy away from truth.

3. We don't spend time meditating on or even reading God's word, so we don't actually know what it says. We either prioritize our lives incorrectly or give in to laziness, causing us to miss making our days primarily about the Lord.

When we fail to get community right it directly hinders our ability to commune with one another. It's incredibly damaging to us if we are attempting to be "*one in heart and mind*" (Acts 4:32) with someone whose heart and mind is not set on Christ alone. But when we get it right, we are able to sharpen one another into men and women after God's own heart (Prov 27:17). That's why it is vital, no matter the cost, for us to fight hard to hold sacred the exclusive body of Christ. Let's spend a bit more time engaging with the benefit of true biblical community because, as we have already discussed, God does not make rules simply to be a rule maker, but because "*in all things God works for the good of those who love him, who have been called according to his purpose*" (Rom 8:28).

In general, there are two types of horizontal relationships (our relationships with other people) we see within the Bible: fellowship (which includes discipleship) with believers, and ministry toward unbelievers. Essentially this boils down to our engagement with those within the church and outside of the church (so long as the church is reserved for the believer). We see this very clearly when we look again at the two paths Jesus describes in Matt 7:13–14: "*Enter through the narrow gate. For wide is the gate and broad is the road that leads to destruction, and many enter through it. But small is the gate and narrow the road that leads to life, and only a few find it.*" Regardless of level of spiritual maturity, if you are born again in Christ you are set on the narrow path toward the narrow gate which leads to life. Conversely, regardless of quantity or severity of sin, those who are not born again in Christ are set on the wide path toward the wide gate that leads to destruction. We as believers are those who were "*bought at a price*" (1 Cor 6:20), who are living within the "*boundless riches of Christ*" (Eph 3:8) and "*whose names are written in the Lamb's book of life*" (Rev 21:27). How then can we think to join in fellowship with those who live in such a way that "*their destiny is destruction, their god is their stomach, and their glory is in their shame. Their mind is set on earthly things*" (Phil 3:19)?

A healthy yielding to the Holy Spirit is key to engaging with the Lord in this area in addition to the exclusivity of the body of Christ becoming evident to us. Consider spiritual gifts given to the believer as laid out in passages such as 1 Cor 12 and Rom 12. These gifts exist within us because the Spirit himself dwells within us as temples, as Paul makes clear in 1 Cor 6:19 when he asks, "*Do you not know that your bodies are temples of the Holy Spirit, who is in you, whom you have received from God? You are not your own.*" How then would it be possible for someone who is not a temple to live out the power that comes from the Holy Spirit? Simply put, they can't. The Bible lays out a framework of an incredibly high standard of living whose conditions can *only* be met by way of the Spirit.

Now, you may be thinking, "Hold on, Trevor. This all seems very harsh and all around unloving toward an unbeliever. What gives?" Imagine for a moment that someone is dying of cancer, and you just discovered the cure. What would be a more loving approach: to try to convince them that they don't have cancer by putting a wig onto their head and makeup onto their downtrodden face to cover up any of their symptoms? Or to acknowledge that they are dying and in need of the cure you found? No one in their right mind would ever think the former route is a loving approach. It's wildly inconsiderate and all around unloving. But that is exactly what we do to someone who is unsaved when we engage with them as if they are saved. We can do no greater disservice to someone than to make them believe they aren't dying and desperately in need of the cure Christ provides. Let our brokenheartedness toward an unbeliever propel us into a deeper pursuit of bringing them to the cross by providing to them the *true* and *full* gospel. Nothing more, nothing less.

Let's take a moment to look at the story of Peter walking on water in Matt 14:22–33, as he was in a similar situation:

> *Immediately Jesus made the disciples get into the boat and go on ahead of him to the other side, while he dismissed the crowd. After he had dismissed them, he went up on a mountainside by himself to pray. Later that night, he was there alone, and the boat was already a considerable distance from land, buffeted by the waves because the wind was against it.*
>
> *Shortly before dawn Jesus went out to them, walking on the lake. When the disciples saw him walking on the lake, they were terrified. "It's a ghost," they said, and cried out in fear.*
>
> *But Jesus immediately said to them: "Take courage! It is I. Don't be afraid."*
>
> *"Lord, if it's you," Peter replied, "tell me to come to you on the water."*
>
> *"Come," he said.*
>
> *Then Peter got down out of the boat, walked on the water and came toward Jesus. But when he saw the wind, he was afraid and, beginning to sink, cried out, "Lord, save me!"*
>
> *Immediately Jesus reached out his hand and caught him. "You of little faith," he said, "why did you doubt?"*
>
> *And when they climbed into the boat, the wind died down. Then those who were in the boat worshiped him, saying, "Truly you are the Son of God."*

Jesus models so beautifully here that he is our Savior, through and through. What if, as Peter is sinking, the other disciples in the boat yelled, "We believe in you, Peter! You have the strength to save yourself and even walk on water!" How differently could this story have ended up being? What if Peter, instead of crying out "*Lord, save me!,*" mustered up all his strength and tried to remain afloat? We would have ended up with a very dead Peter and a different cornerstone that Jesus built the church on. Thankfully, he was aware that there was one way to be saved: surrendering to the Almighty. Likewise, we need to fight tooth and nail to gently and lovingly usher those who are sinking into an understanding that they have to reach out to Jesus to be saved. Telling them that they're fine will only hurt them in the end.

We have spent a large amount of time discussing how to magnify the cross in our lives: the lives of believers. But this is where we are able to make evident the beauty of the cross to unbelievers. It is incredibly misleading to someone trying to understand the crucifixion if they think that there are no stakes to following the Lord. The only way to encounter God in a salvatory way is through surrendering to Jesus on the cross as our bridge back to himself. This is what he meant in John 14:6 when he declares, "*I am the way, and the truth, and the life. No one comes to the Father except through me.*" To inadvertently or intentionally model to someone that they can have the King without the cross is damaging to not only their potential receiving of Christ as Lord (as we have then become a stumbling block) but also to our magnification of Jesus, who paved the only true way to life. There absolutely is a necessity to have tact when engaging with an unbeliever about how they are different from the redeemed, but how it plays out in practice is different from person to person. This again illuminates the importance of being in the presence of God regularly, letting him dictate the pace and direction of your life. Reliance on the Spirit is vital if we want to effectively magnify the cross. At the end of the day, though, it is of utmost importance that we don't weary the Lord by saying "'*All who do evil are good in the eyes of the Lord, and he is pleased with them*' or '*Where is the God of justice?*'" (Mal 2:17).

There are many ways in which creating an environment that endorses exclusivity can and should affect the way we operate. As a brief example and a means of whetting your appetite, examine God's heart for communion as found in Paul's letter to the Corinthian church in 1 Cor 10:21–22 and 1 Cor 11:26–29. The possibilities of practicality are seemingly endless, making this is an aspect of following Jesus that requires reliance on the Spirit. Vigorously study God's word to discern how to healthily create a divide between the sacred and set-apart body of Christ and those who have not yet been grafted into the family of God. Not to push unbelievers away from God, but rather provoke them into his arms.

I want to emphasize the importance of not watering down the cross by looking at how the early 1900s German Lutheran pastor and theologian Dietrich Bonhoeffer approached this aspect of our walk with Christ. He describes the two ways we model Jesus dying for us as either cheap or costly grace. If you've not read his book *The Cost of Discipleship*, I highly encourage you to do so, as it helps to open our eyes to more of what our King has called us to. He begins the book with the statement, "Cheap grace is the deadly enemy of our church. We are fighting to-day for costly grace."[1] He then goes on to explain in detail the difference between the two. He describes cheap grace as follows:

> Cheap grace means grace as a doctrine, a principle, a system. It means forgiveness of sins proclaimed as a general truth, the love of God taught as the Christian "conception" of God. An intellectual assent to that idea is held to be of itself sufficient to secure remission of sins. The church which holds the correct doctrine of grace has, it is supposed, ipso facto a part in that grace. In such a church the world finds a cheap covering for its sins; no contrition is required, still less any real desire to be delivered from sin. Cheap grace therefore amounts to a denial of the living Word of God, in fact, a denial of the Incarnation of the Word of God.
>
> Cheap grace means the justification of sin without the justification of the sinner. Grace alone does everything, they say, and so everything can remain as it was before.[2]

What this essentially boils down to is this: cheap grace means to receive Christ on the cross as a "get out of jail free" card with no requirement to encounter a transformation in the way we live and what we strive for. It belittles the cross. It makes a mockery of the price that Jesus paid for us. For this reason, Jesus himself explains to his disciples that *"whoever wants to be my disciple must deny themselves and take up their cross and follow me. For whoever wants to save their life will lose it, but whoever loses their life for me will*

1. Bonhoeffer, *Cost of Discipleship*, 45.
2. Bonhoeffer, *Cost of Discipleship*, 45–46.

find it" (Matt 16:24–25). If we are to be followers of the true Jesus and not some made-up version of him that we crafted for ourselves so that we feel good, it will require our entire selves. It will require daily surrender of our lives, dying to Jesus, and living like him, with him, and for him. It will require a significant cost. Bonhoeffer describes costly grace as follows:

> Costly grace is the treasure hidden in the field; for the sake of it a man will gladly go and sell all that he has. It is the pearl of great price to buy which the merchant will sell all his goods. It is the kingly rule of Christ, for whose sake a man will pluck out the eye which causes him to stumble, it is the call of Jesus Christ at which the disciple leaves his nets and follows him.
>
> Costly grace is the gospel which must be sought again and again, the gift which must be asked for, the door at which a man must knock.
>
> Such grace is costly because it calls us to follow, and it is grace because it calls us to follow Jesus Christ. It is costly because it costs a man his life, and it is grace because it gives a man the only true life. It is costly because it condemns sin, and grace because it justifies the sinner. Above all, it is costly because it cost God the life of his Son: "ye were bought at a price," and what has cost God much cannot be cheap for us. Above all, it is grace because God did not reckon his Son too dear a price to pay for our life, but delivered him up for us. Costly grace is the Incarnation of God.
>
> Costly grace is the sanctuary of God; it has to be protected from the world, and not thrown to the dogs. It is therefore the living word, the Word of God, which he speaks as it pleases him. Costly grace confronts us as a gracious call to follow Jesus, it comes as a word of forgiveness to the broken spirit and the contrite heart. Grace is costly because it compels a man to submit to the yoke of Christ and follow him; it is grace because Jesus says: "*My yoke is easy and my burden is light.*"[3]

---

3. Bonhoeffer, *Cost of Discipleship*, 47–48.

The model of cheap and costly grace gives us a clearer picture of why it is so important to hold sacred the exclusive body of Christ. The reality of what God did for us is a bit of a paradox and it makes sense why we tend to get it all twisted. Is God's grace upon us free? Yes, as it is written in Rom 6:23, *"For the wages of sin is death, but the free gift of God is eternal life in Christ Jesus our Lord."* But does it simultaneously cost everything? Absolutely. Jesus models this in Mark 10:21 while conversing with the "rich young ruler" when *"Jesus looked at him and loved him. 'One thing you lack,' he said. 'Go, sell everything you have and give to the poor, and you will have treasure in heaven. Then come, follow me.'"*

Brother or sister, hear my plea: Let us be men and women after God who do not fall into the trap of believing we are freed in Christ without a cost, but rather willingly sacrifice everything for his name and daily bind ourselves to his yoke. Only then will we be able to encounter true joy through maximized glorification of his name. And when an unbeliever looks at us, there will be no question as to what it means to be a part of the church of Christ. We are a people set apart from the world. Let us not even for an instant look like the rest of the world around us. And let us never allow the world around us to believe that they can commune with this body without sharing in the sufferings of Christ. As Paul describes in Rom 8:17, *"if we are children, then we are heirs—heirs of God and co-heirs with Christ, if indeed we share in his sufferings in order that we may also share in his glory."* What a beautifully powerful way to magnify the cross in our lives! Christ paid the ultimate price for us, and we in turn give everything joyfully back to him.

Now that we have created a clear distinction between the people of God and those who live for the world, it is important that we navigate internally how to enhance our glorification of the Lord by not being polluted by the world. Let's take some time to look at what it means to truly live apart from sin and cling to the one and only God.

Chapter Ten

The Seriousness of Sin

What shall we say, then? Shall we go on sinning so that grace may increase? By no means! We are those who have died to sin; how can we live in it any longer? Or don't you know that all of us who were baptized into Christ Jesus were baptized into his death? We were therefore buried with him through baptism into death in order that, just as Christ was raised from the dead through the glory of the Father, we too may live a new life.

—Romans 6:1–4

Perhaps the greatest hindrance to our ability to magnify the Lord in our lives is by claiming to be one who has died to sin and yet choosing to continue living in it. Martin Luther once said that "the clergy is the greatest hindrance to faith." I believe this remains to be true both inside and outside the body of Christ. Those who claim to be saved by Jesus' blood but have lives that look identical to the rest of the world make a mockery of the cross. We as the church play a large role in the reason many people believe Christians are hypocrites. My prayer within this chapter is that our eyes would be opened to three things: (1) that we would see clearly how God feels about those who live in patterns of unrepentant sin, (2) how we as brothers and sisters in Christ are called to navigate situations in which a fellow believer is living in sin, and (3) why the fight against sin is necessary to maximize our glorification of the Lord.

As Paul made abundantly clear in Rom 6:1–4, if we truly are those who have been washed by the blood of Christ, born again by the Spirit, and are adopted sons and daughters of the Father, then there is no place for sin in our lives. The apostle John, in 1 John 2:3–6, backed up Paul's claim when he declared, "*We know that we have come to know him if we keep his commands. Whoever says, 'I know him,' but does not do what he commands is a liar, and the truth is not in that person. But if anyone obeys his word, love for God is truly made complete in them. This is how we know we are in him: Whoever claims to live in him must live as Jesus did.*" There isn't much wiggle room within this scripture to live for the world. If I am to live in such a way that the Bible truly is authoritative in my life, then I can be confident that if I am living in unrepentant sin, I can also be confident that I am not actually redeemed in Christ.

This may come off initially as being very harsh, but I hope you will come to see that there is no better way we can love someone who has been lulled to sleep by the enemy than by waking them up from their slumber. What a dreadful day it will be for the exclusively nominal "Christian" (Christian in name alone) when they stand before the Lord on judgment day and read off their "list of good works" and he responds with "*I never knew you; depart from me, you workers of lawlessness*" (Matt 7:23). I believe seventeenth-century theologian John Owen is so right when he calls us to "be killing sin, or it will be killing you."

Now I want one thing to be clear in the midst of this: having sin is *very* different than living in sin. We are by nature sinful beings and will always be imperfect until the day the Lord calls us home, although as we are sanctified by the Holy Spirit the frequency and intensity of our sin should decrease. The sins that exist in our lives that are showered in confession and repentance are those that are pinned to the cross with Jesus as laid out in 1 John 1:9: "*If we confess our sins, he is faithful and just and will forgive us our sins and purify us from all unrighteousness.*" But for those who remain in sin, God has some very pointed truths to declare.

Regarding Israel within their sin:

> "*Because of all their wickedness in Gilgal,*
> *I hated them there.*
> *Because of their sinful deeds,*
> *I will drive them out of my house.*
> *I will no longer love them;*
> *all their leaders are rebellious.*
> *Ephraim is blighted,*
> *their root is withered,*
> *they yield no fruit.*
> *Even if they bear children,*
> *I will slay their cherished offspring.*"
> *My God will reject them*
> *because they have not obeyed him;*
> *they will be wanderers among the nations.* (Hos 9:15–17)

Jesus's words regarding doing what the master tells us to do:

> *The Lord answered, "Who then is the faithful and wise manager, whom the master puts in charge of his servants to give them their food allowance at the proper time? It will be good for that servant whom the master finds doing so when he returns. Truly I tell you, he will put him in charge of all his possessions. But suppose the servant says to himself, 'My master is taking a long time in coming,' and he then begins to beat the other servants, both men and women, and to eat and drink and get drunk. The master of that servant will come on a day when he does not expect him and at an hour he is not aware of. He will cut him to pieces and assign him a place with the unbelievers.*
> *"The servant who knows the master's will and does not get ready or does not do what the master wants will be beaten with many blows. But the one who does not know and does things deserving punishment will be beaten with few blows. From everyone who has been given much, much will be*

demanded; and from the one who has been entrusted with much, much more will be asked." (Luke 12:42–48)

There is an entire book's worth of Scripture depicting how God feels about those who claim to follow the Lord but live in unrepentant sin. But the one thing that remains consistent throughout them all is that there will be great punishment for these people (even greater than those who never knew the Father). How have we been so foggy eyed as to miss how serious this is? This is precisely what Christ came to save us from, yet many who claim Jesus as Lord *"are crucifying the Son of God all over again and subjecting him to public disgrace"* (Heb 6:6). I fear the enemy has done a very good job at convincing unrepentant "Christians" that they are safe where they are. They have completely fallen asleep within their faith and because of that have potentially become a stumbling block to many believers and unbelievers alike.

I've heard it said regarding our faith that "if you're not growing, you're dying." Stagnation doesn't exist in the realm of our walks with the Lord. As Peter declares in 1 Pet 2:2–3: *"Like newborn babies, crave pure spiritual milk, so that by it you may grow up in your salvation, now that you have tasted that the Lord is good."* If my wife, Madison, and I chose to stop giving our newborn daughter, Lauren, milk, she would not simply remain as is. The life of a newborn is hinged on whether or not they receive sufficient nourishment through milk. Likewise, if we don't die to ourselves daily, pick up our crosses, and follow Jesus, we will not simply remain as is. I have seen many people fall away from the Lord simply because over time their faith in Jesus took an increasingly evident backseat in their lives. A dear friend of mine once described this reality through the analogy of paddling upstream in a kayak. The moment I choose to stop paddling is the moment I begin to drift backward. Dear reader, take heart! Do not let the enemy lull you to sleep or else you will surely backslide. Do not believe the lie that you can live in unrepentant patterns of sin and be one with the Lord. And to those who have already dozed off, *"wake up, sleeper, rise from the dead, and Christ will shine on you"* (Eph 5:14).

We as the church have a very important role to play in all of this. While someone else's sin is never on our shoulders, we have a beautiful opportunity to lovingly and truthfully bring a fallen brother or sister back to the foot of the cross once again. The very last thing James included in his letter was to remind us that "*if one of you should wander from the truth and someone should bring that person back, remember this: Whoever turns a sinner from the error of their way will save them from death and cover over a multitude of sins*" (Jas 5:19–20). James is urging us to fight hard to ensure that no brother or sister should fall away from the faith. So, how have you done with that? Have you fallen to one side of the spectrum and refused to call out darkness in someone so as to not offend them? Or maybe you have fallen to the other side of the spectrum and have lived exclusively to rebuke without modeling the love and sacrifice of Jesus. Or maybe you sit somewhere in the middle, engaging healthily in the sharpening of others, all the while modeling Christ's love for his bride.

We previously spoke about God's desire to keep the body of Christ exclusive, protecting it from sin so that he may "*present her to himself as a radiant church, without stain or wrinkle or any other blemish, but holy and blameless*" (Eph 5:27). Now we have the opportunity to navigate what it looks like to partner with the Lord and each other in this endeavor.

A term you may have heard of (and may feel intimidated by) is church discipline. This generally refers to the body of Christ (primarily within the local church) calling a wayward brother or sister higher with the potential for punishment to come into play if there is no repentance. Now I first want to acknowledge that recently our world's view on discipline has become very twisted. It is largely no longer viewed as loving or healthy for a parent to discipline their children or a coach to discipline their players. Over my four years of coaching freshman football at a local high school I witnessed this firsthand. It progressively became more inappropriate to make a player run laps, do push-ups, or the like as it would cause the player to feel bad, which was looked upon as unproductive, uncaring, or harmful. I want to propose to you that holy discipline does quite the opposite to what our culture says discipline does. As King Solomon says in Prov 3:11–12, "*My son, do not despise the Lord's discipline, and do not resent his rebuke, because the Lord disciplines those he loves, as a father the son he delights in.*" Even more than this, the author of Hebrews takes it further after quoting Solomon by adding:

> *Endure hardship as discipline; God is treating you as his children. For what children are not disciplined by their father? If you are not disciplined—and everyone undergoes discipline—then you are not legitimate, not true sons and daughters at all. Moreover, we have all had human fathers who disciplined us and we respected them for it. How much more should we submit to the Father of spirits and live! They disciplined us for a little while as they thought best; but God disciplines us for our good, in order that we may share in his holiness. No discipline seems pleasant at the time, but painful. Later on, however, it produces a harvest of righteousness and peace for those who have been trained by it.* (Heb 12:7–11)

God disciplines us *because* he loves us. Not apart from it. If we want to healthily engage in church discipline as the Bible calls us to, we first have to acknowledge that it is out of our love (and *only* out of our love) for our brothers and sisters that we do so. We yearn for them to know the Lord more intimately and live holy and blameless lives, so we call them up to the standards of the Bible. So, where do we get this idea of church discipline? Well, there's a few places throughout the Bible that clearly lay it out for us, but let's start with the words of Jesus himself in Matt 18:15–20:

> *If your brother or sister sins, go and point out their fault, just between the two of you. If they listen to you, you have won them over. But if they will not listen, take one or two others along, so that "every matter may be established by the testimony of two or three witnesses." If they still refuse to listen, tell it to the church; and if they refuse to listen even to the church, treat them as you would a pagan or a tax collector.*

Truly I tell you, whatever you bind on earth will be bound in heaven, and whatever you loose on earth will be loosed in heaven.

Again, truly I tell you that if two of you on earth agree about anything they ask for, it will be done for them by my Father in heaven. For where two or three gather in my name, there am I with them.

There's a lot here, so let's unpack what Jesus is communicating to us. He is primarily giving us a framework for how to navigate church discipline with one another. First, we bring the sin up to a brother or sister in hopes that they will see the error of their way and repent. Second, if they still don't turn away from their sin, we bring one or two more people in on the conversation. Third, if they still don't repent, we bring them before the church. Finally, if they still are living in their sin, we *"treat them as you would a pagan or a tax collector."* In other words, we treat them as a non-believer. Which, let me be clear, does not justify us treating them poorly, sinfully judging them, or isolating them. Rather, it should increase our brokenheartedness and care over them and increase our yearning for them to come into a fresh encounter with the King. Jesus closes the section by enabling us to trust the spirit in one another as we come into agreement regarding someone's sin.

This seems like a very harsh final response to someone. The thought of having to treat someone as an unbeliever when we have walked alongside them as friends for a long time seems ridiculous. But as Paul says in 1 Cor 5:4–5, *"when you are assembled and I am with you in spirit, and the power of our Lord Jesus is present, hand this man over to Satan for the destruction of the flesh, so that his spirit may be saved on the day of the Lord."* We press into church discipline not because we are being mean and judgy, but rather that the fallen brother or sister will see how serious their sin is and *"may be saved on the day of the Lord."*

I've heard many people claim that approaching someone's sin is judgmental and therefore we shouldn't do it. Unfortunately, this mindset directly goes against what God's word teaches us. Yes, it is sinful to treat someone unrighteously out of malicious judgments.

But Paul actually encourages us to judge those who are part of the body of Christ in 1 Cor 5:12–13 when he says, "*what business is it of mine to judge those outside the church? Are you not to judge those inside? God will judge those outside. 'Expel the wicked person from among you.'*" Let's be clear that this is not sinful judgment as laid out in Matt 7. But rather this is a calling of one another to live up to the standard that the Bible instructs us to emulate. It's waking someone up from their slumber so that they will see their dependance on the Lord. It's so that we can come alongside his prayer to the Philippian church when he says, "*and this is my prayer: that your love may abound more and more in knowledge and depth of insight, so that you may be able to discern what is best and may be pure and blameless for the day of Christ*" (Phil 1:9–10). We cannot love someone well unless it is based on knowledge and insight regarding who they are and where they stand with the Father.

Paul also makes clear that this type of dialogue is meant to be kept within the church. We are not meant to hold nonbelievers to a biblical standard. As we continue to examine God's heart for church discipline, we again see how crucial it is to remain a unified and exclusive body of Christ. How can someone who is not of the redeemed live up to the standard that the Bible says the redeemed need to live up to? In fact, Paul even takes it as far as saying to "*expel the wicked person from among you*"! Those living apart from the Lord are not welcome into the body of Christ. Not because we don't care about them, but precisely *because* we care about them. If I truly love someone, I will inherently want them to know the joy to be had in Christ. If they are living in such a way that hinders this, I will (out of love for them) call them higher.

The enemy desperately wants to cloud our vision regarding seeing how loving a mindset church discipline is. He wants us to believe the lie that following Christ means to just let people live their lives and not ruffle any feathers. If that were true, then why does Jesus himself declare in Matt 10:34–39:

> *Do not suppose that I have come to bring peace to the earth. I did not come to bring peace, but a sword. For I have come to turn*

"a man against his father,
a daughter against her mother,
a daughter-in-law against her mother-in-law—
a man's enemies will be the members of his own
household."

Anyone who loves their father or mother more than
me is not worthy of me; anyone who loves their son or
daughter more than me is not worthy of me. Whoever does
not take up their cross and follow me is not worthy of me.
Whoever finds their life will lose it, and whoever loses their
life for my sake will find it.

How can Jesus, who is love incarnate, carry a sword of division? Well, the Bible is covered with verses such as Isa 26:3 (*"You will keep in perfect peace those whose minds are steadfast, because they trust in you"*) and John 14:27 (*"Peace I leave with you; my peace I give you. I do not give to you as the world gives. Do not let your hearts be troubled and do not be afraid"*). One hard hitting truth of the Bible is that the texts regarding those who have access to true peace (such as the ones above) are only targeted at God's people or those actively following Jesus. You will not find a passage anywhere in Scripture that would lead us to believe otherwise. So what Jesus is doing here in Matt 10 is truly remarkable. He is trying to make a clear distinction between those who are not his people and those who are his people. Out of his love, he doesn't want anyone to be mistaken. You are either in Christ or out of Christ. It will be a dreadful day for anyone who is convinced they know Jesus but do not. They will stand before the Lord on judgment day and hear that they are not welcome into eternal rest. Jesus is modeling a wonderful kind of love by drawing a clear line between those inside and outside the church. That is what church discipline is all about. It is a focus on not allowing someone to have one foot in and one foot out with Jesus because, as we discussed at the beginning of the chapter, that's just not a possibility in God's eyes. Now, we are certainly not Jesus and should not charge into every ministry opportunity, (spiritual) sword in hand, cutting up relationships. But if we are to come alongside the mission of our

Lord, we have to understand the importance behind a separation between the redeemed and the lost.

I don't want to be misleading and cause someone to believe that church discipline is some foolproof way of bringing people back to Jesus. I personally have seen both sides of the coin. I lost one of my dearest friends due to calling a brother out of his sin. He chose to take personal offense to it and distanced himself from me and my fellow brothers in Christ. To this day, he lives apart from the Lord. On a separate occasion, with a different person, my community gained a stronger and more mature brother because we called him out of his sin and didn't let him commune with us for the time being. To this day, he will tell you that being removed from the physical body of Christ is what enabled God to open his eyes to where he had fallen short.

Two very similar accounts with two drastically different results. How can this be? Well, it's because it isn't on our shoulders to bring people into conviction. As Paul explains in 1 Cor 3:6–7, "*I planted the seed, Apollos watered it, but God has been making it grow. So neither the one who plants nor the one who waters is anything, but only God, who makes things grow.*" We as the body of Christ have a great opportunity to partner with the Lord. It's all by God, through God, and for God, yet he is gracious in giving us a role to play. So, brother and sister, plant your seed of church discipline or water another's, but do not grow weary because of what God grows or does not grow. The Father frees us from this pressure.

It's also important that we acknowledge the prerequisite to all of this: introspection. In Matt 7:3–5, Jesus explains to us the dangers of hypocrisy:

> *Why do you look at the speck of sawdust in your brother's eye and pay no attention to the plank in your own eye? How can you say to your brother, "Let me take the speck out of your eye," when all the time there is a plank in your own eye? You hypocrite, first take the plank out of your own eye, and then you will see clearly to remove the speck from your brother's eye.*

Before we can healthily engage in church discipline, we need to first go before the Lord to ensure that we have not lived in any patterns of sin ourselves. How can one blind man lead another blind man to Christ? They can't. As Jesus declares in Matt 15:14, *"they are blind guides. If the blind lead the blind, both will fall into a pit."* So let us be diligent in making sure we are not blind before working to remedy another brother or sister's blindness. In all ways regarding church discipline, let our "Wonderful Counselor" guide our way. Before we dive headfirst into calling someone out, let us be diligently seeking the Lord in prayer. If our hope is to sharpen one another as Prov 27:17 instructs, then let us allow Christ to first prepare in us the tools to use. There are healthy and unhealthy ways to come before a brother or sister who is in sin. Let the King instruct your steps so that when all is said and done, *"[their] spirit may be saved on the day of the Lord"* (1 Cor 5:5).

I pray you are beginning to see how necessary it is to hold true to the exclusive body of Christ by way of church discipline. It's vital if we hope to make the cross bigger in our lives and magnify the Lord in all ways. How can we adequately represent Jesus on the cross if we fail to acknowledge the distinction he died to make? However, when we lovingly live out and model the separation Christ himself created between the redeemed of the Lord and those who live as enemies of his name, people will begin to see how wonderful a savior Jesus can be for them. When Jesus brought his sword to separate humanity in two, he revealed to us the already existing and massive canyon between us and himself. There is only one way to bridge this gap and it is through what Paul explains to the Ephesian church in Eph 3:17-19: *"And I pray that you, being rooted and established in love, may have power, together with all the Lord's holy people, to grasp how wide and long and high and deep is the love of Christ."* The love of Christ, given to us by way of the cross, is the bridge. Let us make it known to all people and in all ways throughout every aspect of our lives, but specifically when it comes to keeping God's people as a holy and set apart people.

Now to you, wayward brother or sister, who are actively engaging in patterns of sin. Here is what I would present to you:

"*A person is not a Jew who is one only outwardly, nor is circumcision merely outward and physical. No, a person is a Jew who is one inwardly; and circumcision is circumcision of the heart, by the Spirit, not by the written code. Such a person's praise is not from other people, but from God*" (Rom 2:28–29). You can attend all the Bible studies in the world, spend countless hours in prayer, daily meditate on the word of God, consistently attend church services, and never truly be of the Lord's redeemed people.

How is your soul doing? Are you wholeheartedly surrendered to God's love and grace? Or do you try to look like a good Christian outwardly because it makes you feel and appear good? As early 1900s preacher Billy Sunday explains, "Going to church doesn't make you a Christian any more than going to a garage makes you an automobile." I plead with you, brother or sister, to turn to the Lord. Lay down your desire to look or feel good and cling to the only true way to life: Jesus. Not the Jesus that you've potentially half-heartedly followed, but the one who calls you by his death to allow himself to be enthroned upon your heart. This is not a matter of merely action and deed, but allegiance and binding. Jesus makes very clear what the person wrapped up in sin is bound to when he declares "*Very truly I tell you, everyone who sins is a slave to sin*" (John 8:34). The reality of the situation is that Jesus on the cross put the key in lock of your chains and freed you. When you engage in sin, all you are doing is closing the bindings around yourself once again. Thankfully, our savior is also "the Great Physician" and has the desire to free you from your bondage to sin. All you have to do is submit to his healing and redemptive process by way of the Spirit. Consider the reality that you are by mere nature of being an image bearer of the Lord designed to be God's beloved son or daughter. But you have chosen to rebel and turn away. God's desire within the seriousness of unrepentant sin is that you would step out of that life and into the loving arms of your Savior under the new covenant given to the redeemed by Jesus's blood. Hear God's call to you in Jer 3:14: "'*Return, faithless people,' declares the Lord, 'for I am your husband. I will choose you—one from a town and two from a clan—and bring you to Zion.'*" Come back and be with your king the way you were originally designed to. He would love for you to rest in his joyous presence.

Now to the believer, Gal 5:1 says that *"it is for freedom that Christ has set us free. Stand firm, then, and do not let yourselves be burdened again by a yoke of slavery."* Perhaps the wildest concept about our freedom is that to truly be free means to bind ourselves to the Lord as his slaves and as his servants. In Phlm 1 Paul refers to himself as *"a prisoner of Christ Jesus."* It even seems paradoxical that Jesus calls us to freedom and then says in Matt 11:29–30 to *"take my yoke upon you and learn from me, for I am gentle and humble in heart, and you will find rest for your souls. For my yoke is easy and my burden is light."* If you're unfamiliar, a yoke is what we put around cattle to bind them to the cart or plow when we need them to do our bidding. The only way to make sense of all this is to accept the reality that if I truly want to be free in this life, I must enslave myself to the Lord, become his prisoner, and allow him to dictate my every step. For *"where the Spirit of the Lord is, there is freedom"* (2 Cor 3:17).

When we actually take the time to investigate God's word, it may seem absurd that we as the church have fallen so short of what God calls us to regarding separation between believer and unbeliever, as well as living above reproach. While yes, our flesh has absolutely hindered our ability to magnify the Lord in these ways, we also have a war being waged on another front. We have an enemy, the devil, who despises us and actively uses his reign on Earth to hinder our glorification of the Lord. It's vital for us to take some time to investigate not only who the devil is, but how he operates and, more importantly, how we can partner with the one true King to rid him of any power he has over us.

Chapter Eleven

The Spiritual War

*Be alert and of sober mind. Your enemy the devil prowls
around like a roaring lion looking for someone to devour. Resist
him, standing firm in the faith, because you know that the
family of believers throughout the world is undergoing the same
kind of sufferings.*

—1 Peter 5:8

*The mind governed by the flesh is hostile to God; it does not
submit to God's law, nor can it do so.*

—Romans 8:7

In hopes of explaining spiritual warfare to my high school self
with fickle theology, an old mentor of mine described spiritual
warfare using an analogy of a light switch enabling us to see the
spiritual realm in which we could observe angels and demons actively waging war over our souls. While this analogy isn't airtight,

it does help to portray the reality of spiritual warfare existing and that it's constant and does not cease to exist simply because I choose to deny its existence. Paul understood this, which is why he fervently explains to the Ephesians to *"be strong in the Lord and in his mighty power. Put on the full armor of God, so that you can take your stand against the devil's schemes. For our struggle is not against flesh and blood, but against the rulers, against the authorities, against the powers of this dark world and against the spiritual forces of evil in the heavenly realms"* (Eph 6:10–12). We are at war whether we like to believe it or not. And to be honest, in my experience, those who refuse to accept the call to enlist in the war are generally the ones who have fallen asleep in their faith. Constantly throughout Scripture we see physical wars break out due to God's people attempting to join in on the spiritual fight. King David himself fought many wars in order to protect God's people and advance the Lord's kingdom. What would have happened if David had refused to believe that Goliath was standing on the doorstep of Israel and didn't go out to fight him? Would it have changed the fact that the enemy was before him? Absolutely not. And we wouldn't have the legendary story of a shepherd boy killing a mammoth of a man with a rock and a sling. Regarding the war within the heavenly realms, our neglect for its existence does not make it any less real or prevalent. That being said, the first step we have to take in magnifying the Lord in the midst of the battle is acknowledgment. We have to acknowledge that there is a fight to be had, pick up a sword, and start swinging.

Every war has at least two sides, and in the case of our spiritual war, there are those who fight for the Lord and those who fight against him. Unfortunately for us, not only do we have satan and his forces of darkness fighting against us, but our very own flesh is also at war with the regenerative work the Spirit is doing within us. Fortunately for us, our God is victorious over all. Thankfully, *"the word of God is alive and active. Sharper than any double-edged sword, it penetrates even to dividing soul and spirit, joints and marrow; it judges the thoughts and attitudes of the heart"* (Heb 4:12). When someone refers to something as a "double-edged sword" they are generally referring to something as having an inherent benefit as well as an inherent pain. The word of God absolutely has both a benefit and a pain within the spiritual war. It benefits us because it is our weapon against the enemy and his forces of evil. It brings "pain" to us because it kills our flesh, leaving space for the Spirit to come in and make his dwelling place. This is vital as it is by the Spirit that we receive the means to be sanctified. I would encourage you, as you continue to navigate your walk with the Lord, to grow in a reliance on the Spirit. Whether by prayer, worship, reading Scripture, or the like, posture yourself to tangibly invite the Holy Spirit in to do a wonderful work in your soul.

The battle against our flesh plays out a bit differently from our battle against the devil, but both are necessary to engage with if we hope to further increase God's glorification in our lives. Let's look a bit deeper into both of these fronts and how we can pick up a sword to fight, *"for though we live in the world, we do not wage war as the world does. The weapons we fight with are not the weapons of the world. On the contrary, they have divine power to demolish strongholds"* (2 Cor 10:3–4).

THE FLESH

> *Those who live according to the flesh have their minds set on what the flesh desires; but those who live in accordance with the Spirit have their minds set on what the Spirit desires. The mind governed by the flesh is death, but the mind governed by the Spirit is life and peace. The mind governed by the flesh is hostile to God; it does not submit to God's law, nor can it do so. Those who are in the realm of the flesh cannot please God.* (Rom 8:5–8)

What Paul is trying to explain to us here is that the flesh operates in direct opposition to the Spirit and that those who live by the flesh are actively living as enemies of God. So, what then actually is the flesh when the Bible talks about it? Surely God is not calling us to go and find a new physical body, right? Well, the flesh simply refers to any piece of us that exists apart from the new creation

God has turned us into as laid out in 2 Cor 5:17 and Gal 2:19–20. The flesh consists of all those humanistic desires we have that don't directly glorify the Lord. The issue lies in the reality that, although we are made new in Christ, our sinful flesh or, our "old man" as the Bible sometimes puts it, still tries to claw its way back into control. This is why we still have impure desires and are drawn to temptation even after receiving Christ. How then do we rectify this? How do we once and for all make a clean break with our old selves and allow the Spirit to be the sole ruler in our hearts? Paul, in Gal 5:16–24, gives us some good insight into this area:

> *So I say, walk by the Spirit, and you will not gratify the desires of the flesh. For the flesh desires what is contrary to the Spirit, and the Spirit what is contrary to the flesh. They are in conflict with each other, so that you are not to do whatever you want. But if you are led by the Spirit, you are not under the law.*
>
> *The acts of the flesh are obvious: sexual immorality, impurity and debauchery; idolatry and witchcraft; hatred, discord, jealousy, fits of rage, selfish ambition, dissensions, factions and envy; drunkenness, orgies, and the like. I warn you, as I did before, that those who live like this will not inherit the kingdom of God.*
>
> *But the fruit of the Spirit is love, joy, peace, forbearance, kindness, goodness, faithfulness, gentleness and self-control. Against such things there is no law. Those who belong to Christ Jesus have crucified the flesh with its passions and desires.*

What is the answer to our previous questions? To "*walk by the Spirit*"! Walking by the Spirit simply means to allow him to dictate your every step through this life. This leaves no room for watering down our sin. Do you justify your sin by claiming you are imperfect or naturally sinful? While yes, we are all imperfect, it's also a cop-out when it comes to walking by the Spirit. Will we all have the ability to sin until the day the Lord calls us home and into perfection? Yes. But as we continue to "*walk by the Spirit,*" sin should inherently have less power in our lives and therefore become less prevalent. To be clear, as one of the redeemed, you are freed from sin and therefore do *not* have to give in to it. But there is grace if you slip up and do. Nevertheless, do not let the flesh win this war because of an apathetic mindset. In fact, John quite boldly reinforces this concept when he declares in 1 John 3:9 that "*no one who is born of God will continue to sin, because God's seed remains in them; they cannot go on sinning, because they have been born of God.*"

Brother or sister, please hear me say this with much love: you are no longer seen in God's eyes as sinners, but saints. Let us therefore give way to the Spirit to enable us to act as such. It is for this reason Paul says to:

> *Count yourselves dead to sin but alive to God in Christ Jesus. Therefore do not let sin reign in your mortal body so that you obey its evil desires. Do not offer any part of yourself to sin as an instrument of wickedness, but rather offer yourselves to God as those who have been brought from death to life; and offer every part of yourself to him as an instrument of righteousness. For sin shall no longer be your master, because you are not under the law, but under grace.* (Rom 6:11–14)

As we navigate this aspect of the war before us, let us not forget that the battle is not won on our strength, but God's. Do we have a role to play? Yes, but it is simply to move aside and to "*not quench the Spirit*" (1 Thess 5:19). Give him the space to do the work he is already doing within us.

THE DEVIL

> *And no wonder, for Satan himself masquerades as an angel of light. It is not surprising, then, if his servants also masquerade as servants of righteousness. Their end will be what their actions deserve.* (2 Cor 11:14–15)

I want to begin this section by breaking down a couple of myths regarding satan. First and foremost, it's likely not satan or his demons that causes you to stumble every time you give way to sin. A large part of the time this is actually just our sinful flesh attempting to claw its way back onto the throne as we just spoke about. Additionally, satan is not omnipresent like our Lord. He exists in one place and at one time. So, for example, when you are being attacked with fear and anxiety, it is most likely not the devil himself, but rather his servants. He is, although, the king of this world for the time being and has many demons under his command who do in fact attack us. We see this at its extreme in the many instances where demonic possession exists in the Bible (see Mark 1:21–28, Matt 8:28–34, Luke 11:14–28, and Mark 7:24–30 for examples).

The devil exists for one reason alone: to harm God's creation. As John 10:10 describes, he is *"the thief [that] comes only to steal and kill and destroy."* The devil has existed from the start to work toward hindering our joy and will continue to do this until our King's decisive victory over him as laid out in the book of Revelation. We know this to be true because of what John says in 1 John 3:8: *"The one who does what is sinful is of the devil, because the devil has been sinning from the beginning. The reason the Son of God appeared was to destroy the devil's work."* When Christ graciously came and conquered death for you it began the devil's demise, and praise God that, through John, he gave us hope for what is to come in Rev 12:7–12:

> Then war broke out in heaven. Michael and his angels fought against the dragon, and the dragon and his angels fought back. But he was not strong enough, and they lost their place in heaven. The great dragon was hurled down— that ancient serpent called the devil, or Satan, who leads the whole world astray. He was hurled to the earth, and his angels with him.
>
> Then I heard a loud voice in heaven say:
> "Now have come the salvation and the power
> and the kingdom of our God,
> and the authority of his Messiah.
> For the accuser of our brothers and sisters,
> who accuses them before our God day and night,
> has been hurled down.
> They triumphed over him
> by the blood of the Lamb

and by the word of their testimony;
they did not love their lives so much
as to shrink from death.
Therefore rejoice, you heavens
and you who dwell in them!
But woe to the earth and the sea,
because the devil has gone down to you!
he is filled with fury,
because he knows that his time is short."

We see here that God has already won once when he cast the enemy out of Heaven, and satan knows that he is coming again to deal the final blow. In essence, the devil is trying to do as much damage as he can before his expiration date comes. Even though God will bring final victory soon, we still have a fight on our hands today. So how do we combat him in this present time? We suit up for battle.

Earlier we briefly discussed Paul's call to put on the armor of God, but he elaborates to help us practically understand how to do this. Let's take a look at Eph 6:10–17 to discern how to effectively win the daily battle against the enemy:

Finally, be strong in the Lord and in his mighty power. Put
on the full armor of God, so that you can take your stand
against the devil's schemes. For our struggle is not against
flesh and blood, but against the rulers, against the authori-
ties, against the powers of this dark world and against the
spiritual forces of evil in the heavenly realms. Therefore put
on the full armor of God, so that when the day of evil comes,
you may be able to stand your ground, and after you have
done everything, to stand. Stand firm then, with the belt of
truth buckled around your waist, with the breastplate of
righteousness in place, and with your feet fitted with the
readiness that comes from the gospel of peace. In addition
to all this, take up the shield of faith, with which you can
extinguish all the flaming arrows of the evil one. Take the
helmet of salvation and the sword of the Spirit, which is
the word of God.

It's important that we unpack the various pieces of gear that the Lord provides to us. I pray you begin to see how vital each piece of equipment is as we approach the battle and that if we fight with even one piece missing, we are dangerously vulnerable:

Belt

Truth: *"with the belt of truth buckled around your waist."* I don't think it's any coincidence that the first piece of equipment Paul lists is focused on truth. The Bible says that *"a time is coming and has now come when the true worshipers will worship the Father in the Spirit and in truth, for they are the kind of worshipers the Father seeks. God is spirit, and his worshipers must worship in the Spirit and in truth"* (John 4:23–24). Additionally, in a prayer to the Father in John 17:17, Jesus explains what truth is: *"Sanctify them by the truth; your word is truth."* What these two texts teach us is that we cannot have a right relationship with God unless we come before him in truth and understanding that God's word alone is truth. Therefore, I cannot adequately worship God unless I am under full submission to his word: the Bible. Have you fallen into the snare of the "know your truth" movement we see in society today? Have you either intentionally or unintentionally supported someone's brokenness by allowing them to believe that their thoughts and emotions are truth? If someone's "truth" is anything other than exactly what God has laid out for us in his guidebook to life (the Bible), then it simply isn't truth. Truth is not a spectrum, it is binary. Something is either true or it is not. And if we believe this, then we can be confident that if something is not directly of God's word (truth), it is 100 percent not of truth.

A belt is primarily used as a means of holding clothes together. Without one, my pants are at risk of falling down and my shirt coming untucked. Likewise, truth is the glue that holds everything together for us. That is why it is so important to hold the Bible as infallible and authoritative in our lives. If I struggle to submit to the truth of God's word, I will begin to bend the Bible to be whatever I want it to be, which is wildly dangerous to our understanding of who our King is.

You may be tempted to believe that this is not so black and white. While yes, things other than God's word may be "true" (the grass is green, two plus two equals four, *The Lord of the Rings* is the greatest saga of all time, etc.), there can only ever be one *truth*. Paul drives this point home by declaring at the end of Rom 14:23 that *"everything that does not come from faith is sin."* Therefore, if it is not of the Father, it is entirely not of the Father. Paul then further elaborates on the dangers of swaying away from the truth in 2 Thess 2:9–12:

> *The coming of the lawless one will be in accordance with how Satan works. He will use all sorts of displays of power through signs and wonders that serve the lie, and all the ways that wickedness deceives those who are perishing. They perish because they refused to love the truth and so be saved. For this reason God sends them a powerful delusion so that they will believe the lie and so that all will be condemned who have not believed the truth but have delighted in wickedness.*

Let us be men and women who are held together by the one and only truth that is God's word.

Breastplate

Righteousness: *"with the breastplate of righteousness in place."* It's no mystery as to what a breastplate is used for when it comes to bodily protection. It directly guards most of our vital organs, and most importantly, our heart. King Solomon was one of the wisest (if not the wisest) men to ever live (as described in 1 Kgs 4:29–34), so in Prov 4:23 when he declares, *"above all else, guard your heart, for everything you do flows from it,"* we can be confident that he knows what he is talking about. So, what is Paul trying to communicate is our way of protecting our heart? Righteousness. The dictionary definition of righteousness is "the quality of being morally right or justifiable." As we have discussed in earlier chapters, goodness and morality are held exclusively in the hands of God, and I can certainly not be justified in and of myself. To rectify this, I've heard righteousness defined as "right-with-ness," or the posture of being "right with God." What Paul is ultimately trying to say to us is that the key to guarding our heart is being in right standing with the Lord.

So, how are you doing in your intimacy with the Father? First and foremost, have you been justified by the blood of his Son? Have you received the Holy Spirit and are actively submitting to his authority and power? Beyond that, is your heart postured to *"hate what is evil; [and] cling to what is good"* (Rom 12:9)? We cannot even begin to protect our hearts unless we are in a right relationship with God. As we know through Rom 3:10–20, doing this on our own is a futile effort:

> *As it is written:*
> *"There is no one righteous, not even one;*
> *there is no one who understands;*
> *there is no one who seeks God.*
> *All have turned away,*
> *they have together become worthless;*
> *there is no one who does good,*
> *not even one."*
> *"Their throats are open graves;*
> *their tongues practice deceit."*
> *"The poison of vipers is on their lips."*
> *"Their mouths are full of cursing and bitterness."*
> *"Their feet are swift to shed blood;*
> *ruin and misery mark their ways,*
> *and the way of peace they do not know."*
> *"There is no fear of God before their eyes."*
>
> *Now we know that whatever the law says, it says to those who are under the law, so that every mouth may be silenced and the whole world held accountable to God. Therefore no one will be declared righteous in God's sight by the works of the law; rather, through the law we become conscious of our sin.*

Upon initial inspection, this may seem very bleak. Is Paul trying to communicate to us that our heart will forever be exposed to damage? Absolutely not! Beloved saint, be encouraged by Paul's follow-up in Rom 3:21–26:

> But now apart from the law the righteousness of God has been made known, to which the Law and the Prophets testify. This righteousness is given through faith in Jesus Christ to all who believe. There is no difference between Jew and Gentile, for all have sinned and fall short of the glory of God, and all are justified freely by his grace through the redemption that came by Christ Jesus. God presented Christ as a sacrifice of atonement, through the shedding of his blood—to be received by faith. He did this to demonstrate his righteousness, because in his forbearance he had left the sins committed beforehand unpunished—he did it to demonstrate his righteousness at the present time, so as to be just and the one who justifies those who have faith in Jesus.

Our heart's protection is sure so long as we cling to Christ on the cross. Our righteousness comes exclusively by way of Jesus and not from anything you or I can do on our own. This takes so much pressure off our shoulders in our pursuit of the Lord. We can trust that as we daily surrender to the King and pick up our cross to follow him we are being grown in righteousness by the Spirit he caused to dwell in us.

Boots

Gospel of Peace: "*and with your feet fitted with the readiness that comes from the gospel of peace.*" Something I love to do is hike in beautiful places as I feel very intimately close to God in the midst of his creation. I will be the first to tell you that if you try to travel any longer distance on the ground other than on a sidewalk, good boots are a necessity. In a worldly battle it is vital to be able to move long distances quickly and without hindrance. Likewise, in our spiritual battle, it is crucial to remain in forward motion, never growing stagnant, and never backsliding. Praise God that he equips us with the perfect boots for the job.

The word *gospel* comes from the Greek word for "good news." So "the gospel of peace" can be translated then to "the good news of peace." If we take it even further, in Col 3:15 Paul says to "*let the peace of Christ rule in your hearts, since as members of one body you were called to peace,*" proving to us that the peace we seek is Christ himself. If we smash all of this together, we find that "the gospel of peace" will translate to "the good news of Jesus"! So, the equipment that enables our feet to move onward is none other than the person of Christ. It is for this reason that Paul declares that "*Christ's love compels us, because we are convinced that one died for all, and therefore all died*" (2 Cor 5:14). I am *compelled* by Christ to do the work he died to enable me to do.

Dear brother or sister, do not let anything other than Jesus himself be the fuel that drives you forward. Every seemingly legitimate substitute will always run dry before the finish line. We have discussed at length the importance of making the Lord the centerpiece of our story, and this is a prime way to engage in that truth. If we hope to truly live out the Great Commission, spreading the gospel and making disciples for his name, it must be done on the grounds of Christ enabling our steps by the boots he equips us with. My hiking boots will need to be repaired or replaced regularly throughout my life. Thank the Lord that the boots he provides to us (Jesus's redemptive work on our behalf) will last without decay all the way up until we meet him face to face.

Shield

Faith: "*In addition to all this, take up the shield of faith, with which you can extinguish all the flaming arrows of the evil one.*" As Paul explains in Eph 6, the enemy is constantly firing flaming arrows our way. Readying a shield is the perfect way to fend off his volley. It may seem superfluous to have to have a shield at all. We have been discussing all different kinds of armor that are designed to protect from the enemy, so why have a shield as well? While it is true that these different pieces of armor will save you from an enemy's attack, a shield is designed to be the first line of defense. I won't get into the physics of it, but taking a blow off the armor attached to your body still transfers much of the blunt force directly into your body, which does not feel good. A shield, since it is attached to two hinges (your shoulder and elbow), has much more room to negate the force of the attack, causing much less trauma to the body.

When I played football growing up, we would run drills where one player would hit another player who was holding a big shield made of high-density foam. With the shield the defending player would hardly feel a thing when the attacking player made contact. If, for some odd reason, the defending player decided to stand there with just his football pads and take on the full force of the attacking player's hit to his body he would still feel much of the blow, even though his pads would protect from some of the damage. I hope you see the point here: a soldier without a shield can still walk away greatly bruised and beaten. But one who wields their shield well can come out of battle unscathed.

We can translate this to understanding the importance of having faith. Let's take a look at a battle with the devil that Jesus himself encountered and how he defended himself:

> *Then Jesus was led by the Spirit into the wilderness to be tempted by the devil. After fasting forty days and forty nights, he was hungry. The tempter came to him and said, "If you are the Son of God, tell these stones to become bread."*
>
> *Jesus answered, "It is written: 'Man shall not live on bread alone, but on every word that comes from the mouth of God.'"*
>
> *Then the devil took him to the holy city and had him stand on the highest point of the temple. "If you are the Son of God," he said, "throw yourself down. For it is written:*
>
> *'he will command his angels concerning you,*
> *and they will lift you up in their hands,*
> *so that you will not strike your foot against a stone.'*
>
> *Jesus answered him, "It is also written: 'Do not put the Lord your God to the test.'"*

> *Again, the devil took him to a very high mountain and showed him all the kingdoms of the world and their splendor. "All this I will give you," he said, "if you will bow down and worship me."*
>
> *Jesus said to him, "Away from me, Satan! For it is written: 'Worship the Lord your God, and serve him only.'"*
>
> *Then the devil left him, and angels came and attended him.* (Matt 4:1–11)

Jesus models here two very important aspects of our battle with the enemy: faith-based defense and Scripture-based attack. Now, I won't get into the Scripture piece here as that is coming up shortly, but Jesus models a faith that is crucial for us to emulate. He just finished spending forty days and nights without food, and as the Bible says, "*he was hungry.*" If you've ever fasted before for any duration, you will know that there comes a time where you're not just hungry, you're *hungry*. The feeling transcends a desire for food and becomes an overwhelming feeling of weakness throughout the body. That is likely what Jesus is encountering here, but to the nth degree. This is where faith becomes a wonderful shield. It didn't matter what the devil threw his way. Jesus was confident that the Father was sufficient for him. He was convinced that nothing would satisfy him the way the King would.

I encourage you to take some time to examine Heb 11 when you get the chance, as it is often referred to as the "Hall of Faith" for a good reason. The author lists out example after example of biblical figures who modeled great faith. What is interesting is that they begin the chapter by saying that "*faith is confidence in what we hope for and assurance about what we do not see*" (Heb 11:1) and ends it by saying that "*these were all commended for their faith, yet none of them received what had been promised, since God had planned something better for us so that only together with us would they be made perfect*" (Heb 11:39–40). What these biblical accounts show us is the power of having full confidence in the promises of God, even if we don't see them come to fruition in our lifetime. So, if I am stricken with illness, debilitated by injury, or crippled with depression, and the enemy comes with an offer that seems pretty good, I can hold up my shield of faith and cling to God's promise in Jer 33:6 when he says, "*behold, I will bring to it health and healing, and I will heal them; and I will reveal to them an abundance of peace and truth*" and again in 2 Cor 12:9: "*my grace is sufficient for you, for my power is made perfect in weakness.*"

Although we may not see the physical manifestation of God or his promises this side of Heaven, our confidence in who he says he is and what he will do will be sufficient enough faith to protect us from the fiery arrows of our King's opposer.

Helmet

Salvation: "*Take the helmet of salvation.*" Here's a fun fact about the human brain: it's essentially Mary Poppins's bag of limitless capacity. Research has shown that there are around one hundred billion neurons in our brains that all receive, process, transmit, and store information. These neurons then make connections with one another to add up to around one quadrillion connections, which all store and send data. That's a whole lot of information! I'm fascinated by the fact that God created these oddly shaped blobs in our heads to be an infinite playground for knowledge and learning. I don't think then that it's a coincidence that Paul says to use "*the helmet of salvation*" to protect this treasure trove.

The brain is arguably the most important organ (alongside the heart) for good reason. It enables us to accomplish anything from something as simple as breathing or eating to something as complex as falling in love, creating fantastical stories, or furthering scientific discoveries. If even one part of the brain is damaged, a bodily or mental function will cease to operate. Our brains are what give us the ability to make informed decisions in life. Jesus knew this, which is why he discussed the matter of salvation in this way:

> No one can come to me unless the Father who sent me draws them, and I will raise them up at the last day. It is written in the Prophets: "They will all be taught by God." Everyone who has heard the Father and learned from him

comes to me. No one has seen the Father except the one
who is from God; only he has seen the Father. Very truly
I tell you, the one who believes has eternal life. I am the
bread of life. Your ancestors ate the manna in the wilder-
ness, yet they died. But here is the bread that comes down
from heaven, which anyone may eat and not die. I am the
living bread that came down from heaven. Whoever eats
this bread will live forever. This bread is my flesh, which I
will give for the life of the world. (John 6:44–51)

As we can see from the text, salvation exists exclusively within the person of Jesus as someone is drawn in by the Father. But what may be easier to miss is the emphasis on learning and decision making. Now I want to be clear about something upfront: This is not a dissertation on the validity or invalidity of predestination and free will. This is hopefully just an analysis of what God's word explicitly says. I will leave the rest up to you and the Holy Spirit to hash out together. For as Paul says in Phil 2:12–13: "*Therefore, my dear friends, as you have always obeyed—not only in my pres-ence, but now much more in my absence—continue to work out your salvation with fear and trembling, for it is God who works in you to will and to act in order to fulfill his good purpose.*"

After we are drawn in by the Lord, we enter into this space of being "*taught by God,*" believing in who he says he is, and eating of the "*bread that came down from heaven.*" All three of these aspects are rooted in choices that we make within our own brains. And all three of these things should happen in the order that Jesus lays out for us here. God's heart as he draws us to himself is that we would yearn for him in these specific areas. As for being "*taught by God,*" my wife is a teacher and would be the first to tell you that just because someone instructs doesn't mean that someone listens to, much less learns, what is instructed. The constant battle for her as a teacher is ushering the students to have a posture that enables them to learn what is to be taught. But at the end of the day, the students need to decide for themselves that it is worth it to learn. Likewise, we need to posture ourselves to hear, receive, and learn from the Father. In Phil 1:9–11 Paul prays "*that your love may abound more and more in knowledge and depth of insight, so that you may be able to discern what is best and may be pure and blameless for the day of Christ, filled with the fruit of righteousness that comes through Jesus Christ—to the glory and praise of God."* What Paul has ascertained is that our ability to walk out an active and abundant life with Christ is hinged on having *"knowledge and depth of insight."* This knowledge then fuels belief.

When you sit down in a chair, do you take time beforehand to investigate the sturdiness of the legs or discern how the physics acting on the joints will work? No, you most likely do not. That is because your general knowledge and experiences surrounding chairs drives your belief that they will hold you up if you sit in them. In the same way, having been taught by God himself, we are able to believe in who he really is, and not some version you, I, or some other person dreamed up. Belief without knowledge is a faulty belief as it has no foundation or backing in truth. And as we already discussed, something is not of truth unless it is of the Lord. This is precisely what Paul is addressing in Rom 10:14 when he asks, *"how, then, can they call on the one they have not believed in? And how can they believe in the one of whom they have not heard? And how can they hear without someone preaching to them?"* We are unable to truly believe in Jesus unless we have heard and learned of what he did for us on Calvary. And as this verse mentions, belief is the prerequisite to engaging with the King.

The final piece to the puzzle is eating the *"bread that came down from heaven."* It's the daily act of surrendering to the reality that we need Christ as our daily sustenance. But as we have now seen, this is based on the prerequisites of learning from the Father and believing in his name. We choose when we eat and what we eat. We choose to diet. We choose to indulge. We choose to take the bread of life and eat it as Christ calls us to do. Believer, you have been called by the Father; now make the decision based upon knowledge and belief to eat of the bread he provides for you.

We do not receive salvation by way of the brain, as it is *"by grace you have been saved, through faith—and this is not from yourselves, it is the gift of God—not by works, so that no one can boast"* (Eph 2:8–9). But salvation is directly linked to the brain and is therefore out to protect it. Salvation by way of the cross is what guards my ability to learn from the Father, believe in Jesus's body and blood, and fill my body with the bread of life that is received through the Spirit. So, don salvation as your helmet and make the daily choice to run earnestly into the good and loving arms of your Father.

Sword

God's Word: *"and the sword of the Spirit, which is the word of God."* As we just discussed, our brains have virtually unlimited storage capacity. So why then do we struggle to daily walk with *"the sword of the Spirit, which is the word of God"*? Joshua 1:8–9 provides an interesting perspective into how we should engage with God's word when it says to *"keep this Book of the Law always on your lips; meditate on it day and night, so that you may be careful to do everything written in it. Then you will be prosperous and successful. Have I not commanded you? Be strong and courageous. Do not be afraid; do not be discouraged, for the Lord your God will be with you wherever you go."*

The quality in which we follow the Lord can never and will never be based upon results, but humbly asking ourselves questions about what we have been doing for the sake of God's glory is a good way of taking inventory of our hearts as we can know a person's heart (ourselves included) based on their fruit, as Jesus explains in Matt 7:15–20:

> *Watch out for false prophets. They come to you in sheep's clothing, but inwardly they are ferocious wolves. By their fruit you will recognize them. Do people pick grapes from thornbushes, or figs from thistles? Likewise, every good tree bears good fruit, but a bad tree bears bad fruit. A good tree cannot bear bad fruit, and a bad tree cannot bear good fruit. Every tree that does not bear good fruit is cut down and thrown into the fire. Thus, by their fruit you will recognize them.*

That being said, how have you done within your walk with the Lord as it pertains to memorizing his word? God does not tell Joshua to "keep this Book of the Law always in your eyes," but rather to *"keep this Book of the Law always on your lips."* Spending time reading God's word is amazing, and will grow you in wonderful ways, but don't miss God's instruction. The Bible is meant to be always on our lips. The only way we can do this is by storing it in the infinite knowledge bank that is our brain. In a part of a sermon where he lists off many of the benefits to memorizing Scripture, John Piper explains one benefit that is vital to adequately engage within this spiritual war:

> Memorizing Scripture enables me to hit the devil in the face with a force he cannot resist to protect myself and my family from his assaults. What are you hitting him with? He is millions of times stronger than you, and he hates you, and your family, and your marriage, and this church, and God. How anybody walks through this devil ruled world without a sword in their hand is beyond me.[1]

Previously, in the section talking about the shield of faith, we discussed how Jesus in the wilderness used faith and Scripture as his defense and attack in his battle against the enemy. Jesus did not carry around a "pocket Bible," he did not cling to "Christianese" ideologies that he had heard, and he certainly did not have a smartphone with a web browser at his fingertips. No, Jesus had God's law written onto his heart, loaded in the chamber, ready to fire at a moment's notice.

I'll never forget the first verse I memorized: 1 Cor 10:13. I was early in my faith and was still learning how to put to death the sinful urges of my old self, and in this case, specifically relating to lust and pornography. I had grown to understand rather quickly that on my own strength, I stood no chance against either the flesh nor satan and his demons. So, I wrote this verse onto my heart, and whenever I would feel tempted, I would recite, *"No temptation has overtaken you except what is common to mankind. And God is*

1. Piper, "Your Deadliest Weapon."

faithful; he will not let you be tempted beyond what you can bear. But when you are tempted, he will also provide a way out so that you can endure it." Was this a foolproof way to win the battle? No, as that is why we previously spoke about faith and the necessity to surrender to the King. But did it help me to actively speak truth over myself and reroute my gaze back to the cross? Absolutely. Don't let the enemy lull you into a belief that memorizing Scripture is not vital or a direct instruction from the Lord. It requires work, so our lazy flesh will resist it, but when we put in the time to invest in the memorization of God's word, we can confidently say, "*I have stored up your word in my heart, that I might not sin against you*" (Ps 119:11).

As Eph 6 makes clear, Scripture is our sword and our weapon in this war. Do not wait until the enemy is standing before you to scramble to find a weapon. Brandish it now, so that when the time comes, you are ready to do as James instructs in Jas 4:7: "*Submit yourselves, then, to God. Resist the devil, and he will flee from you.*" Don't be overwhelmed by this call but be encouraged through your heart for God. How many songs or movie quotes do you have cached in your brain? You likely remember them because of your love or enjoyment for those pieces of media. Now if we memorize media due to the enjoyment they bring, how much more should we submit to memorizing the very words of our King, who is our first love and ultimate joy? Brother or sister, humble yourself to take baby steps. Maybe this week you will commit to memorizing one verse, and a couple new verses the next. Before you know it, you will have a whole host of God's wonderful words imprinted on your heart and you will be ready to wield your sword in the face of battle.

As we near the close of this chapter, I want to address what many people fall into when it comes to spiritual warfare: passivity. We began this chapter with 1 Pet 5:8, which says to "*Be alert and of sober mind. Your enemy the devil prowls around like a roaring lion looking for someone to devour. Resist him, standing firm in the faith, because you know that the family of believers throughout the world is undergoing the same kind of sufferings.*" So, we find ourselves here with a lion, the king of the jungle, a formidable and dangerous opponent, waiting for his opportunity to strike, and yet we so frequently act like he's either not there or we try to pet him and train him to do our bidding. It's utter foolishness. Let's take a look at what the Village Church's pastor Matt Chandler had to say on this subject in his sermon titled "Grace Driven Effort":

> Every now and then, there is a show on the Discovery Channel called "When Animals Attack." Have any of you ever seen this? I absolutely love the show. Nine times out of ten, I'm cheering for the animal. I just want to be straight with you. And in one scene, it was these guys fishing in a canoe in Alaska and this grizzly just charges them. And I just thought, "I mean what do you do?" Um, pray. That's what you do. You've got a fishing rod and you're in a canoe when here comes an apex predator. The second one was this company wanting to sell watches and had this really beautiful model come and lay down with this lion, and then the lion attacked her. I'm like, "Yeah, because it's an apex predator. That's what they do. They kill everything else. Nothing hunts a giant male lion. The giant male lion hunts everything. If they get hungry enough in packs, they'll hunt like elephants and giraffes. They are apex predators." So, I say this, if you put enchiladas in front of me, I am eventually going to eat them. Maybe not tonight. Maybe I gorged myself on queso and chips beforehand. Maybe I had salsa or some guacamole. Maybe I'm just not in the mood, but eventually I am going to eat the enchiladas. And on this night, the lion turns and eats the girl, and everyone is like, "This is crazy!" No, it's really not. You just laid some enchilada on him. He was hungry and he ate. So, here's what happens. We have a little pet sin, and we think we've got it controlled. Then it turns on us and destroys us and we are thinking, "This is crazy. Where did this come from? How did this happen?" Well, you gave quarter to something that you can't really control in the end. And for all the bravado, "I've taught him to sit. I've taught him to roll over. I've taught him to beg. I've taught him to shake. I've taught him to speak." For all the "I've controlled him,"

it only takes the right circumstance or the right setting for him to turn and do what he was created to do, which is deceive you and destroy you and kill you and lie to you. You buy in, and you're right back to square one. So, grace-driven effort is violent because it understands that the lion is out to destroy. The lion is seeking someone to devour. The man of the house understands that if he is devoured, there are other people that are wounded by him being devoured. There is collateral damage to his failure as a man. So, he puts the lion down. He doesn't just starve him; he starves him to death. He doesn't strike him once; he strikes him and strikes him and strikes him and will not quit hitting until he's dead. Grace-driven effort is violent. I think some of the reasons that a lot of you have been stuck in frustration for a long time is that you are simply not violent enough towards your sin.[2]

Dearly beloved brother or sister, we are at war with an enemy we stand no chance against on our own accord. If we truly hope to glorify the Lord as much as possible, we have to daily engage in this battle, and the only way to adequately do so is by putting on our Eph 6 "armor of God" and cutting the head off the lion, whether that lion be our flesh or the devil himself. An army's armor will generally have the sigil or crest of their nation and their king imprinted onto it. Bear the crest of your King, the cross, with honor. This battle will surely end when Christ returns, but for now, fight in such a way that you bring glory to your King and "*magnify the Lord.*"

You may be wondering how to practically "*fight the good fight of the faith*" as Paul urges us to do in 1 Tim 6:12. Well, a good place to start is where Jesus ended: the Great Commission.

---

2. Chandler, "Grace Driven Effort."

Chapter Twelve

The Call to Ministry

All authority in heaven and on earth has been given to me.
Therefore go and make disciples of all nations, baptizing them
in the name of the Father and of the Son and of the Holy Spirit,
and teaching them to obey everything I have commanded you.
And surely I am with you always, to the very end of the age.

—Matthew 28:18–20

WHAT IS THE THING you love most in the world outside of Jesus? Is it your family? Is it your friends? Or perhaps your job? Maybe it's a hobby such as hiking, working out, or reading books. Now think for a minute about the amount of time throughout a typical day you think about this one thing. Now think for another minute about how much time is spent talking to others about this one thing or even engaging with others in it. I would venture to guess that it takes up a good percentage of your social conversation, mental capacity, and physical activity on any given day. As Jesus himself says in Luke 6:45: "*A good man brings good things out of the good stored up in his heart, and an evil man brings evil things out of the evil stored up in his heart. For the mouth speaks what the heart is full of."*

When my daughter, Lauren, was born, I was (and still am) in awe of God's unbelievably beautiful creation. I did not know I could love something so small so much. I had to work hard to not exclusively talk about her to everyone I came in contact with in hopes of not being "the parent who only ever talks about their kids." Now, we as Christians have our entire being in submission to our Lord out of an abundance of love for him. Do we have an eagerness to talk about our love for the King the way we do for our children? Do we struggle to keep our love and excitement about Jesus contained because we can't help but do as the psalmist, Ethan, explains in Ps 89:1: *"I will sing of the Lord's great love forever; with my mouth I will make your faithfulness known through all generations"*?

The apostles Peter and John had an encounter where their lives were at risk from the same people who had just recently killed Jesus simply because they healed someone in need. Yet as you will see, they were so infatuated with the Father that their response to their oppressors was simply, *"As for us, we cannot help speaking about what we have seen and heard"* (Acts 4:20). Let's take a look at the full account in Acts 4:1–20 and observe how this scenario came about:

> *The priests and the captain of the temple guard and the Sadducees came up to Peter and John while they were speaking to the people. They were greatly disturbed because the apostles were teaching the people, proclaiming in Jesus the resurrection of the dead. They seized Peter and John and, because it was evening, they put them in jail until the next day. But many who heard the message believed; so the number of men who believed grew to about five thousand. The next day the rulers, the elders and the teachers of the law met in Jerusalem. Annas the high priest was there, and so were Caiaphas, John, Alexander and others of the high priest's family. They had Peter and John brought before them and began to question them: "By what*

power or what name did you do this?" Then Peter, filled with the Holy Spirit, said to them: "Rulers and elders of the people! If we are being called to account today for an act of kindness shown to a man who was lame and are being asked how he was healed, then know this, you and all the people of Israel: It is by the name of Jesus Christ of Nazareth, whom you crucified but whom God raised from the dead, that this man stands before you healed. Jesus is 'the stone you builders rejected, which has become the cornerstone.' Salvation is found in no one else, for there is no other name under heaven given to mankind by which we must be saved." When they saw the courage of Peter and John and realized that they were unschooled, ordinary men, they were astonished and they took note that these men had been with Jesus. But since they could see the man who had been healed standing there with them, there was nothing they could say. So they ordered them to withdraw from the Sanhedrin and then conferred together. "What are we going to do with these men?" they asked. "Everyone living in Jerusalem knows they have performed a notable sign, and we cannot deny it. But to stop this thing from spreading any further among the people, we must warn them to speak no longer to anyone in this name." Then they called them in again and commanded them not to speak or teach at all in the name of Jesus. But Peter and John replied, "Which is right in God's eyes: to listen to you, or to him? You be the judges! As for us, we cannot help speaking about what we have seen and heard."

I fear that many of us exist in a space quite the opposite to this. We are often timid and scared and flee from opportunities to speak his name in a public (or even private) setting. A question I ask myself is: How can I adequately live out the Great Commission from Matt 28:18–20 if I am too frightened to go on "*speaking about what [I] have seen and heard*"?

Have you ever wondered why God chose to leave believers on Earth once they were saved rather than beam them up into Heaven? We know it's possible because (1) God is infinitely powerful and can do as he pleases, and (2) he did exactly that to Elijah when he and Elisha were walking and this miraculous occurrence happened: "*As they were walking along and talking together, suddenly a chariot of fire and horses of fire appeared and separated the two of them, and Elijah went up to heaven in a whirlwind*" (2 Kgs 2:11). The reason God doesn't beam us up is because of the same reason we spoke about in the beginning of this book: we exist for God's glory. The end goal is not solely to come to know the Lord in intimacy. It is to fall in love with the Lord and allow that passion to spill out into a drive to make disciples of the nations. This truly is the pinnacle of our glorifying the King. Bringing him maximized praise is found in the Great Commission.

A friend of mine once said that there is only one thing we can do for the Lord on Earth that we can't do in Heaven: preach the gospel to lost souls. We have the cure for a disease more serious than cancer and we struggle to administer it out of fear of being looked down upon or being judged. It seems so silly on paper but, as we all have likely encountered, there is a very real resistance to freely proclaiming the gospel to those who are spiritually and physically dying.

Famous magician and self-proclaimed atheist Penn Jillette once described his frustrations with Christians in a video wherein he said (for context, to "proselytize" means to try to convert someone):

> I've always said I don't respect people who don't proselytize. I don't respect that at all. If you believe there is a heaven and hell, and people could be going to hell or not getting eternal life or whatever, and you think it's not really worth telling them this because it would make it socially awkward. . . . How much do you have to hate somebody to not proselytize? How much do you have to hate someone to believe everlasting life is possible and not tell them that? If I believed, beyond a shadow of a doubt, that a truck was coming at you, and you didn't believe it, that that truck was bearing down on you, there's a certain point that I tackle you, and this is more important than that.[1]

1. Jillette, "Not Proselytize."

I find it wildly sobering to know that choosing to not preach the gospel in word and deed is to actively choose to work against the gospel as explained in Rom 10:14–15: "*How, then, can they call on the one they have not believed in? And how can they believe in the one of whom they have not heard? And how can they hear without someone preaching to them? And how can anyone preach unless they are sent? As it is written: 'How beautiful are the feet of those who bring good news!'*" Brother or sister, please hear this: if you are of the redeemed then you have already been sent by Jesus when he declared, "*Peace be with you! As the Father has sent me, I am sending you*" (John 20:21). You have already been called, according to Paul in Rom 8:28–30: "*And we know that in all things God works for the good of those who love him, who have been called according to his purpose. For those God foreknew he also predestined to be conformed to the image of his Son, that he might be the firstborn among many brothers and sisters. And those he predestined, he also called; those he called, he also justified; those he justified, he also glorified.*" And you have already been given the authority to carry the good news, as we ourselves are walking manifestations of it according to 1 Cor 6:19: "*Do you not know that your bodies are temples of the Holy Spirit, who is in you, whom you have received from God?*"

While yes, it's true that even "*if [we] keep quiet, the stones will cry out*" (Luke 19:40), God has chosen us as his beloved children, rather than some pebbles, to be the mouthpiece for his gospel to the nations. What a wonderful gift it is that God, in his abundant grace, has given us the opportunity to experience the joys of proclaiming the good news of his name to the lost and broken people of the world!

In the past when I have had conversations with people about the practicalities of ministry, I have noticed a lot of people, myself included, get very hung up on how it should flow or tangibly play out. They get lost in the details. When we examine God's word (specifically in the New Testament, as ministry looked rather different in the Old Testament), we see that there are really only two avenues that people take regarding reaching the lost: long-term relationship-based and short account-based ministry. Ideally, we model both of these types of ministry regularly, as that is how Christ modeled it. Nevertheless, let's unpack these two styles a bit.

When I say long-term relationship-based ministry, I am referring to what many people nowadays would refer to as discipleship, or the process of intentionally growing someone into a disciple of Christ. This would look like any relationship in which we regularly engage with someone in hopes of them growing in their faith and love of Christ. In college I was a volunteer for the youth ministry organization Young Life. This style of ministry is what my time there was generally spent on. I was placed at a local high school where I spent years developing relationships with students, preaching the gospel to them, and walking alongside them as they grew in the Lord. Jesus himself models relational ministry in many encounters, but I want to look deeper into his relationship with Matthew to get a better picture of how this plays out.

THE CALLING OF MATTHEW (MATTHEW 9:9–13)

> As Jesus went on from there, he saw a man named Matthew sitting at the tax collector's booth. "Follow me," he told him, and Matthew got up and followed him.
>
> While Jesus was having dinner at Matthew's house, many tax collectors and sinners came and ate with him and his disciples. When the Pharisees saw this, they asked his disciples, "Why does your teacher eat with tax collectors and sinners?"
>
> On hearing this, Jesus said, "It is not the healthy who need a doctor, but the sick. But go and learn what this means: 'I desire mercy, not sacrifice.' For I have not come to call the righteous, but sinners."

As we dive in, it's important to note that tax collectors were generally not well thought of people. They would often require people to pay higher than accurate taxes and then take the excess for themselves. They were looked at with disfavor and, as the Pharisees pointed out, are generally referenced alongside sinners. What Jesus initially models here is the beauty of the reach of the gospel.

No one is outside of God's sovereignty, and we should never assume someone is "too far gone." That sort of condemnation and judgment is reserved for God alone as laid out by Paul in 1 Cor 5:12–13: "*What business is it of mine to judge those outside the church? Are you not to judge those inside? God will judge those outside. 'Expel the wicked person from among you.'*" Our job is to plant the seeds of God's word into the soil of people's hearts. It's not to discern which ones should or shouldn't grow.

We see that the relationship Jesus began here with Matthew grew into something remarkable as Matthew was selected to be an apostle and even (likely) went on to write his own Gospel! To elaborate, this was just one discipleship relationship of at least seventy-two (or seventy in certain manuscripts) where Jesus models this type of ministry. Matthew was later intentionally chosen to be one of the twelve apostles.

The life of Matthew perfectly depicts a relationship-based ministry as it shows the commitment Jesus made to walking alongside Matthew as a disciple. Jesus was able to watch his disciple walk away from his life of sin and cling to the King. This relationship lasted roughly three years as Jesus then went to the cross. In our lives, this may look like investing relationally in a coworker, roommate, old or new friend, family member, etc. This is a very powerful form of ministry but is resource limited. Unfortunately, time is finite, and in order to intentionally live out Paul's charge to "*follow my example, as I follow the example of Christ*" (1 Cor 11:1), then we have to be prayerful about discerning who God desires for us to devote time to building disciple-centric relationships with. Thankfully, the Bible models another form of ministry to fill the void left by lack of time.

Short account-based ministry is any encounter we may have with people that does not remain for the long haul. Praying for someone random, preaching the gospel in front of a crowd, or discussing God's goodness with the family at the table next to you during dinner are all forms of short account ministry. This type of ministry exists in both the micro and macro sense. Let's examine first the micro side of things. When I say micro, I mean when the ministry is done to a single person (or perhaps a small group of people). It's more personal and intimate and allows for us to home in on the needs of the individual. Philip models short account ministry in the micro sense very clearly in this encounter with an Ethiopian eunuch.

PHILIP AND THE ETHIOPIAN (ACTS 8:26–39)

Now an angel of the Lord said to Philip, "Rise and go toward the south to the road that goes down from Jerusalem to Gaza." This is a desert place. And he rose and went. And there was an Ethiopian, a eunuch, a court official of Candace, queen of the Ethiopians, who was in charge of all her treasure. He had come to Jerusalem to worship and was returning, seated in his chariot, and he was reading the prophet Isaiah. And the Spirit said to Philip, "Go over and join this chariot." So Philip ran to him and heard him reading Isaiah the prophet and asked, "Do you understand what you are reading?" And he said, "How can I, unless someone guides me?" And he invited Philip to come up and sit with him. Now the passage of the Scripture that he was reading was this:

"Like a sheep he was led to the slaughter
and like a lamb before its shearer is silent,
so he opens not his mouth.
In his humiliation justice was denied him.
Who can describe his generation?
For his life is taken away from the earth."

And the eunuch said to Philip, "About whom, I ask you, does the prophet say this, about himself or about someone else?" Then Philip opened his mouth, and beginning with this Scripture he told him the good news about Jesus. And as they were going along the road they came to some water, and the eunuch said, "See, here is water! What prevents me from being baptized?" And he commanded the chariot to stop, and they both went down into the water, Philip and the eunuch, and he baptized him. And when they came up out of the water, the Spirit of the Lord

> *carried Philip away, and the eunuch saw him no more, and*
> *went on his way rejoicing.*

I believe that the key to micro short account ministry is found when "*Philip opened his mouth, and beginning with this Scripture he told him the good news about Jesus.*" To effectively minister in a short account to a small group of people, it is vital "*that your love may abound more and more in knowledge and depth of insight*" (Phil 1:9). Jesus similarly models this mindset in his encounter with the Samaritan woman at the well in John 4:1–26. We can clearly portray the gospel of Christ to someone by knowing how to effectively communicate it to them. The content and quality of the gospel we preach can never be anything less than the fullness of God's word, but the method in which we relay it to the unbeliever can be malleable as even Christ himself preached the same truth in multiple different ways when interacting with different people. Maybe it happens through a tear-filled night of intentional conversations. Or maybe through a casual conversation alongside some chips and salsa. Or maybe the gospel is clearly portrayed through a carefully crafted written letter. This kind of ministry is wonderful in our ability to present the gospel to many people in a more consistent manner throughout our days. The caveat would be to ensure that we don't water down God's truth for the sake of brevity, as this can lead to false beliefs on the side of the listener if left up to their own interpretations.

Finally, we come to the macro model of short account ministry. This would arguably be what brought about the largest gospel growth in the early days of the church. We see this very commonly throughout the New Testament from anyone from Jesus (Sermon on the Mount) to Paul (the numerous times he's arrested for preaching the gospel to crowds) and, as we will now examine, to Peter (at Pentecost).

PETER AT PENTECOST (ACTS 2:22-41)

"Fellow Israelites, listen to this: Jesus of Nazareth was a man accredited by God to you by miracles, wonders and signs, which God did among you through him, as you yourselves know. This man was handed over to you by God's deliberate plan and foreknowledge; and you, with the help of wicked men, put him to death by nailing him to the cross. But God raised him from the dead, freeing him from the agony of death, because it was impossible for death to keep its hold on him. David said about him:

> *'I saw the Lord always before me.*
> *Because he is at my right hand,*
> *I will not be shaken.*
> *Therefore my heart is glad and my tongue rejoices;*
> *my body also will rest in hope,*
> *because you will not abandon me to the realm of the dead,*
> *you will not let your holy one see decay.*
> *You have made known to me the paths of life;*
> *you will fill me with joy in your presence.'*

"Fellow Israelites, I can tell you confidently that the patriarch David died and was buried, and his tomb is here to this day. But he was a prophet and knew that God had promised him on oath that he would place one of his descendants on his throne. Seeing what was to come, he spoke of the resurrection of the Messiah, that he was not abandoned to the realm of the dead, nor did his body see decay. God has raised this Jesus to life, and we are all witnesses of it. Exalted to the right hand of God, he has received from the Father the promised Holy Spirit and has poured out what you now see and hear. For David did not ascend to heaven, and yet he said,

> *'The Lord said to my Lord:*
> *"Sit at my right hand*
> *until I make your enemies*
> *a footstool for your feet."'*

"Therefore let all Israel be assured of this: God has made this Jesus, whom you crucified, both Lord and Messiah."

> *When the people heard this, they were cut to the heart and said to Peter and the other apostles, "Brothers, what shall we do?"*
>
> *Peter replied, "Repent and be baptized, every one of you, in the name of Jesus Christ for the forgiveness of your sins. And you will receive the gift of the Holy Spirit. The promise is for you and your children and for all who are far off—for all whom the Lord our God will call."*
>
> *With many other words he warned them; and he pleaded with them, "Save yourselves from this corrupt generation." Those who accepted his message were baptized, and about three thousand were added to their number that day.*

We see here that Peter boldly stands before a large crowd of people and preaches the gospel directly from God's word. This led to around three thousand people turning to follow Jesus that day. Peter's ministry here is macro because it involves a lot of people, and it's based on short accounts because Peter surely doesn't have the capacity to engage in intimate fellowship with each of these new believers. This happens multiple times throughout Scripture, and tens of thousands of people are documented to have begun following Jesus because of this type of ministry. What an incredible work God has historically done through this avenue! The difficulty here is that, when not dealt with carefully and exclusively biblically, it can lead to people misunderstanding what is being said or even being hurt by what is preached. In college, I remember seeing people exhibiting this kind of ministry in our public quad where thousands of students would venture through between classes. Many times, I would be encouraged as they unapologetically preached Christ from God's word. Other times, I was heartbroken as the preacher pushed a subjective agenda that was not biblically sound and caused listeners to walk away frustrated or saddened. This shows us the need for reliance upon the Holy Spirit and the Bible. God's word has many hard truths for people who preach a gospel other than the one Jesus died to give us.

I am incredibly grateful that God has provided the model for three very different and yet very practical forms of ministry. As we near the close of this journey, I want to illuminate the importance of your individual and unique ministry. No Christian is called to take a backseat role in this life. In light of the coming hardships, Paul declares in Acts 20:24: "*I consider my life worth nothing to me; my only aim is to finish the race and complete the task the Lord Jesus has given me—the task of testifying to the good news of God's grace.*" Paul had the understanding that he existed to further God's glory, specifically through the proclamation of the gospel in ministry. As we discussed when we examined his "road to Rome," Paul was given a very clear mission from the Lord: "*As you have testified about me in Jerusalem, so you must also testify in Rome*" (Acts 23:11). Your mission, believer, is one and the same. You exist to "*finish the race and complete the task the Lord Jesus has given [you].*" Your primary motive in life must be to elevate your King and to bring him more glory. Ministry is perhaps one of the most powerful avenues to do so.

As an aside, do not be fooled into thinking that our words are the only means of doing ministry and bringing people to the feet of Jesus. When the apostle John calls us by saying, "*Dear children, let us not love with words or speech but with actions and in truth*" (1 John 3:18), he is urging us to live lives that directly point back to Jesus in every way. Take time to process your life and the way you live. Does every aspect of your life honor the Lord? Does every aspect magnify his name? As John makes clear in 1 John 1:6, "*If we claim to have fellowship with him and yet walk in the darkness, we lie and do not live out the truth.*" Everything you do, everything you say, and everything you think is all a part of your ministry back to the Lord. If it isn't furthering the advancement of his glory, it is likely standing in the way of it.

Amid this calling the Lord has given us, he is gracious in allowing us to further our joy by partaking in his ministry. This is what Paul models in Phil 4:1 when he says, "*Therefore, my brothers and sisters, you whom I love and long for, my joy and crown, stand firm in the Lord in this way, dear friends!*" There truly is no greater joy apart from Christ himself and our magnification of him than watching a lost soul become one of the redeemed. Jesus himself agrees with the joys of ministry when he says, "*I tell you that in the same way there will be more rejoicing in heaven over one sinner who repents than over ninety-nine righteous persons who do not need to repent"* (Luke 15:7). Let your life be marked by an individual passion for the Lord that wells up into a yearning to expand his kingdom to the masses for the sake of his glory.

Epilogue

The Son is the image of the invisible God, the firstborn over all creation. For in him all things were created: things in heaven and on earth, visible and invisible, whether thrones or powers or rulers or authorities; all things have been created through him and for him.

—Colossians 1:15–16

THIS INTRO SCRIPTURE IS incredibly powerful in circling us back to the foundation of this book: we exist for God. There is a temptation to read the surrounding context of these verses (which are directly about God caring for his past, current, and future people) and think that it means that the people are the focal point. As the apostle Peter points out in 1 Pet 3:18: *"For Christ also suffered once for sins, the righteous for the unrighteous, to bring you to God. He was put to death in the body but made alive in the Spirit."* While, yes, God's people are the vehicle in which he chooses to exhibit his love and grace, the motivation behind Christ suffering was for the purpose of bringing us into the fold of God which, as we have examined throughout the course of this book, is for his glory. There is no greater joy to be found in life than by allowing ourselves to exist for his magnification. Christ on the cross is the apex of this reality. He is the beginning, and he is the end.

So then, we've now pieced together the puzzle. This is where we "land the plane," so to speak. As we have examined throughout the course of this book, God yearns for us to have a maximized life. The model in which he explains we can have this is through glorification of himself. There's no possibility this book could mention every way to magnify the Lord, but I'll end here with confidence that the Holy Spirit, our helper, will do a lot of the heavy lifting inside of us. As we move on from here, let our heart's beat be that of the psalmist David, in Ps 34:1–10:

> *I will bless the Lord at all times;*
> *his praise shall continually be in my mouth.*
> *My soul makes its boast in the Lord;*
> *let the humble hear and be glad.*
> *Oh, magnify the Lord with me,*
> *and let us exalt his name together!*
> *I sought the Lord, and he answered me*
> *and delivered me from all my fears.*
> *Those who look to him are radiant,*
> *and their faces shall never be ashamed.*
> *This poor man cried, and the Lord heard him*
> *and saved him out of all his troubles.*
> *The angel of the Lord encamps*
> *around those who fear him, and delivers them.*
> *Oh, taste and see that the Lord is good!*
> *Blessed is the man who takes refuge in him!*
> *Oh, fear the Lord, you his saints,*
> *for those who fear him have no lack!*
> *The young lions suffer want and hunger;*
> *but those who seek the Lord lack no good thing.*

My prayer for you as you go:

Father, edify this reader as they seek to honor you to a greater degree. Would you take their desire for you and fan the flame in their soul. Would they rise each morning and lay each night with their eyes fixated on you alone. Further transform the way that they live in and view the world, that they would be a light in the darkness. Bring glory to your name, for this is what we exist for. We love you. To you be the glory, now and forever. Amen.

Bibliography

Bonhoeffer, Dietrich. *The Cost of Discipleship*. Translated by R. H. Fuller. New York: Scribner, 1949.

Carson, D. A. *The Difficult Doctrine of the Love of God*. Wheaton, IL: Crossway, 2000.

Chandler, Matt. "Grace Driven Effort." June 6, 2010. https://www.thevillagechurch.net/resources/sermons/grace-driven-effort.

Jillette, Penn. "Not Proselytize." YouTube video, Nov 13, 2009. https://www.youtube.com/watch?v=owZc3Xq8obk.

Lewis, C. S. "The Poison of Subjectivism." In *Christian Reflections*, 72–81. UK: Eerdmans, 1967.

Piper, John. "Christian Hedonism." Desiring God. https://www.desiringgod.org/topics/christian-hedonism#.

———. "Satan Always Asks Permission: Seven Ways God Reigns over Evil." Desiring God, Aug 31, 2018. https://www.desiringgod.org/messages/the-fall-of-satan-and-the-victory-of-christ/excerpts/satan-always-asks-permission.

———. "Your Deadliest Weapon against the Devil." Desiring God, Aug 9, 2017. https://www.desiringgod.org/messages/if-my-words-abide-in-you--2/excerpts/your-deadliest-weapon-against-the-devil.

Index

Index

Index

Index

Index